mathewson

Oregon Ski Tours

(65 Cross-country Ski Trails)

By Doug Newman and Sally Sharrard

THE TOUCHSTONE PRESS
P.O. Box 81
Beaverton, Oregon 97005

I.S.B.N. No. 0-911518-18-5
Copyright ©1973 by
Doug Newman and Sally Sharrard
Printed in the United States of America.

introduction

This book is dedicated to ski touring as it is practiced in the Oregon Cascades. Primarily, it is designed to introduce you to the ski touring opportunities which exist within a few hour's drive of the state's major population centers.

Within the past five years, ski touring has developed in popularity from an activity practiced by a relative few to something that is capturing the imagination of Americans across the country. Simplicity is probably the key to the sport. Touring is very adaptable. It can be anything you care to make it. It is suitable for families with small children who want a short outing of an hour's duration. It also can be an extended physical experience for those who want to ski many miles over rough terrain on trips lasting several days.

Cross-country skiing in the sense of this book—ski touring as opposed to Nordic racing competition—is a sport for the independent individual. Ski touring is not an exact sort of thing. This book is not an exact sort of thing.

There are several explanations for the lack of explicitness. Three primary reasons are weather, the nature of the activity and the skill levels of the participants. Nothing is constant in a winter environment. With the fall and melt of snow, routes change in length and difficulty, trails vanish, signs are obscured, and parking fluctuates. Depending on the weather and the skier's ability, a short trip can take hours or, conversely, many miles may be covered in a brief period of time.

As this book progressed, attempts to grade or rate trails and individuals in terms of "beginner, intermediate, expert" proved unwieldy and ineffectual. Many things beyond the simple mastery of techniques are combined to establish a person as a competent ski tourer.

Such a person must be able to demonstrate his ability to cope with various problems encountered throughout the tour. These include route finding, evaluation of weather, waxing, proper equipment selection, ability to fix broken equipment, and the ability and willingness to cope with any emergency situation which may arise.

An advanced tourer, in our estimation, is a person at home and comfortable in a winter environment, secure in his knowledge and in his ability to negotiate himself through all terrain and situations without dependence on other tourers or outside individuals or organizations. This aptitude, coupled with the philosophy of freedom and independence, embraces the root appeal of the sport.

Ski touring, as practiced in the Cascades of Oregon, has developed in a way different from that which appears to be evolving in other regions across the country. Thus far, few commercial interests are promoting the activity as it seems now to be promoted in the Rockies and on the east coast. In those locales, while individuals do tour independently, a host of more formal developments have emerged. Ski areas are appealing to the masses with groomed trails, guide services and patrolled routes generally centered in a downhill area with the idea of bringing the skier back to the lodge for lunch.

In Oregon the vast majority of ski tourers are far more independent. Not only are there few guides, there is no touring patrol and few lodges for lunch. Tourers are self-reliant, depending upon their own skills and the resources carried with them in a given tour party.

Oregon ski touring is not for those who seek the manicured track or the helicopter ride to the top of the hill. In that vein, this book is not to be taken as the final, ultimate, up-to-the-minute report on trails, routes, waxing or snow conditions. Its purpose is that of providing suggestions on appropriate places to go. Consequently, we have made an assumption: you will accept this work as but one part in the total picture of successful touring. We will offer clues, hints, advice from our experience and help you on your way. The rest is up to you. Good touring!

contents

how to use this book

For the ski tourer, trip planning—the art of selecting a site and getting there —is perhaps as important as the type of bindings or the kind of wax to use. Many items are involved in its accomplishment.

The first step is to select a tour.

Because of the ever-changing nature of the winter environment, attempts to rate trails in terms of difficulty have proven ineffective. The only distinction made is between tours which are conducted for the most part on *roads* (roads being routes passable by four-wheeled vehicles during summer months) and those which are primarily on *trails* (routes impassable except by foot). In the few cases where roads or trails are not used, a descriptive phrase of the terrain is substituted. Distances listed in trail summary are average round trip unless otherwise noted, and will depend on snow conditions. Caution: a short trail is not necessarily an easy tour.

Unless otherwise stated, road tours are best suited for the beginner. Roads are broader and lack the dips, brush and tight turns of trails, yet they can provide an exhilarating downhill run with a good track, steep grade or icy conditions, but minus the fast turning maneuvers often required of trail skiing.

On this basis, then, the first step is to decide your skill level and start out with tours appropriate to your ability. With only a few exceptions, the vast majority of tours are located on national forest land. Determine national forest, ranger district and U.S. Geological Survey Quadrangle for the tour.

While a map is presented with each tour, for practical purposes it is a good idea to acquire a suitable library of maps covering the areas which you most often visit. Quadrangles are available at stores and on order from the U.S. G.S. and though they are somewhat out-of-date in terms of roads and trails their information is still accurate concerning landforms and drainages.

Along with the quadrangles, you can get a second group of maps—Work Maps or Fireman's Maps by name— free from the U.S. Forest Service. They are best obtained from the ranger station administering the area you are visiting. These maps, updated annually, show the latest in road and trail developments and also the sites of recent logging operations.

A third type of map, a specialty item, is also available from the Forest Service at no charge showing lands within the boundaries of each of the designated wilderness areas.

With the maps assembled, you are now ready to make the trip.

Use an Oregon highway map to get to the general vicinity of your tour site. In mid-winter, under normal conditions, the chance of logging roads above 2,500 feet being open is questionable. If the site you select is off the main, all-weather roads, a telephone call to an appropriate ranger station during office hours is often a good source of information.

Once you arrive at the trailhead, use the Forest Service maps and the quadrangles interchangeably for the rest of the tour to chart your progress. In fact, when you leave the main highway, unless you know the area, an updated Forest Service map is almost essential to assure your taking the correct route on the approach to the trailhead. The contour map, while somewhat dated, still shows the lay of the land and can be particularly helpful when six feet of snow has obscured trails and blazes.

While most people begin touring in the company of other more experienced tourers, the time eventually arrives when skill levels increase and the new skier begins to try new touring sites on his own. As you attempt more complex tours, the following considerations come into play concerning tour selection:

a.) Strengths and skill levels of ALL party members.
b.) Weather—Is it snowing in area? Road conditions. Freezing level. Weather forecast.
c.) Terrain—Is it steep, flat, rolling?
d.) Exposure—If it is spring, will there definitely be snow on exposed south slopes?
e.) Possible Dangers—storms, bad cornices, stream crossings, avalanche possibilities, bad ice on lakes, whiteout conditions.

Planning a ski tour is not a magical feat. It is simply a matter of summoning resources, evaluating your potential strengths and weaknesses and then starting out. With each experience gained, skills are sharpened and the winter world opens for further exploration.

EQUIPMENT LIST

In addition to skis, boots, bindings and poles, the following are items that every ski tourer should carry each time he goes out. These things and the knowledge of their use will enable you to be independent of the group, to take care of yourself without being a burden on others, and to spend a night out in relative comfort should you be delayed in returning from a tour.

Waxes—green, blue, purple, red and yellow tins (yellow Klisterwax is handy for Oregon snow); red and blue Klister; and a small square of paraffin for fast descents.
Waxing cork—compressed cork or styrofoam models.
Scraper—the plastic type with the Klisterwax will suffice.
Repair kit—small stubby screwdriver, small pliers, wooden match sticks, 2 feet of light wire, a few appropriate screws, 6 inches of welding rod, 10 or more feet of nylon cord, tape, metal ski tip, and extra binding parts such as Jofa side cleats and Tempo cables.
Sun glasses and sun lotion.

Flashlight—a small Mallory, with extra batteries and bulb, is perfect.
Waterproof matches, candle and firestarter.
Knife—pocket or Swiss Army.
Map of the area and compass—know how to use them.
Whistle—small police type.
First Aid kit—commercial, ready-made kits ARE NOT RECOMMENDED. Make your own with:

1. roll of 1" adhesive tape
2. moleskin, 4 x 5" or larger
3. a few assorted bandages and gauze pads
4. roll of 1" sterile gauze
5. Ace bandage, 2" width
6. compress with tails (Carlisle Bandage) (2)
7. antiseptic liquid soap
8. aspirin or similar
9. triangular bandage (2)
10. emergency sun glasses
11. razor blade
12. salt tablets
13. ammonia inhalent
14. Boric acid ointment for snow-blindness
15. wire splint

Extra mittens—wool army mitten liners are excellent.
Warm clothing—stocking cap, extra sweater or parka (in pack for when stopping).
Toilet Paper—in plastic sack.
Personal medication items—pills, medications, etc.
Heavy duty space blanket or poncho—with grommet holes.
Lunch, extra food (high energy items) and water.

The importance of being prepared for every tour must be stressed,especially if you are going alone. Carrying the above items helps, but the knowledge of how to utilize all aspects of the environment to your best advantage is more important than equipment. With this in mind, we recommend two very excellent books on general and winter survival: *The Sierra Club Manual of Ski Mountaineering*, Edited by D. Brower, and *How to Stay Alive in the Woods* by Bradford Angier. A very good investment for those interested in first aid would be: *Mountaineering Medicine* by Dr. Fred Darville, *Emergency Medical Guide* by J. Henderson, and *Hypothermia: Killer of the Unprepared* by T. G. Lathrop, M.D.

A final note: shop around before you buy equipment. The things you buy should be practical rather than fashionable. Solicit many opinions and assume a questioning attitude. As the popularity of ski touring increases the prices go up, and the good deals are few and far between.

Remember that the basic philosophy of ski touring is one of independence. There are no ski patrols to sweep dramatically to the rescue at the slightest mishap, and though mountain rescue services do exist, they may be slow in getting organized, and it is often a matter of days before a search can be effective. Winter, while holding much in the way of beauty, serenity and grandure, brooks little nonsense from the ill-prepared or unwary.

This, then, is the reason for such items as emergency ski tips, first aid kits, wire, screws and pliers. A broken ski, 10 miles in powder snow from your car, with no way to fix it, can be a very serious problem.

The prudent tourer is prepared.

WAXING

Other books are devoted exclusively to the subject of touring skills and techniques, including waxing. Rather than describe waxing in total (better done by the technique books), we will briefly highlight those points pertinent to touring in the Cascades.

Oregon snow creates some basic problems. It is not that Oregon is a bad place to tour—it's that Oregon's snow is not usually the virgin powder of colder climes. Consequently, the use of "warmer" waxes is more frequent.

Of all possible waxing problems, one is totally avoidable. Many people mess themselves up by attempting to predict the type of wax they will need before leaving home, applying the chosen wax there and then driving 60 to 100 miles to the touring site. Such guesswork is folly. Nine times out of ten the prediction is wrong and much time and energy is spent scraping off the wrong wax.

The best possible procedure, for those who must putter and pre-wax skis at home, is to make sure the base on your skis is ready for any condition. You can accomplish this by first burning off old waxes and wiping the bottom clean. Then pine-tar the bottoms if they need it. Third, apply a coat of green wax, the hardest wax for the coldest conditions, and melt it on in an even layer. With a base of green you are ready for anything. A kicker of the right consistency can be added in the field for adequate traction and the green base will somewhat protect the tar base if it is abrasive snow.

When you first put on the day's waxes in the field, the safest procedure is to second-guess yourself on how warm you think conditions are. For example: if you guess the wax for your kicker to be red, put on the next coldest wax, purple. Then ski around a little. If you slip too much, put on a little red. It is easier to put wax on than to take it off. If you had not put on purple and the red had been too sticky then a scrape-off job would have been needed.

Some final thoughts to remember: during the day, particularly in the spring, powder can turn to slush. Hence, waxes must be changed. Carry them with you. As you go up in elevation, the quality of the snow will be different. It will also be different if you go from sun to shade or from a southern to a northern exposure. The wax will work differently in those areas. Do not expect too much of your wax. The most important thing to remember about waxing, particularly in climbing, is that good technique will do more toward getting you to the tops of hills than all the wax in the world.

hazards, special techniques & woodsy lore

Cross-country ski touring is a total experience. It is not merely a speedy Saturday afternoon recreational diversion to be clicked on and off. It is a complete interaction with the natural environment on a purely physical basis. Therein lies the beauty.

Ski touring—to Americans, the late-discovered cousin to hiking and mountaineering—offers a unique physical challenge in that it pits man against the natural elements in a setting little known in today's world. While some people insist on battering winter into submission under the clutching treads of an endless variety of roaring, fuming, mechanical monsters, ski tourers prefer to meet nature on her own terms, interact with her for a time and then depart, back to the frustrations of our technological society.

Once the fundamentals of the activity have been mastered, a natural tendency on the part of the fledgling tourer is progression toward more complex winter skills. Learn to live in the woods in the winter and you are competent to travel the same territory at other seasons in style and comfort. Winter travel and life in a winter wilderness environment are the ultimate challenge.

In developing proficiency for winter travel, it is best to participate in the appropriate activity with individuals known to be skilled in these matters. There is no magic formula. Skill is gained by going time and time again, ever alert to the activities of others and the happenings of nature in the world around you.

Before you start out, however, you need some basic clues to appropriate actions and, once they are understood, they can be expanded upon. The following problems and conditions are examples of the obstacles which you will meet in the winter wilderness and which must be overcome:

Avalanches —
Avalanches are a very complex subject about which much has been written. A text, available from the U.S. Forest Service, gives excellent information. The low-level tourer, who only makes occasional forays into avalanche areas, must keep alert for such things as: open slopes, particularly those with cornices above them; signs of previous avalanches such as run-outs; and great fluctuations in temperature that could create varying layers of snow which might not adhere well and would slide. Don't cross suspicious areas in closely-spaced groups. Spread out and use an avalanche cord. Stay in the trees when possible.

Cornices —
Cornices are found usually on ridge tops or any place where wind is common and snow can blow and be drifted. The major effect is that the wind blows snow from one side of the ridge to the other and then extends the snow outward creating a broad, flat expanse which looks solid but which actually is undercut. Don't ski or walk out on ridges which may have cornices and do not ski under cornices.

Crevasses —
Unless you are touring in high mountains, crevasses in the glacial sense are not generally a problem in Oregon. Anyone contemplating spring skiing on a number of glaciers, notably in the Three Sisters area or possibly Mt. Hood, would be well advised to either know the area or to take up the safety devices of the mountaineer: ski roped and use an ice axe, prussik sling and other suitable equipment for travel in a crevassed area.

For the tourer, however, there are several threats of a crevasse-like nature—call them crevices if you will—which may befall the unwary. Tree-wells are one. Another type of hazard is when you walk around on foot after having removed your skis. Falls can become more likely when you are crossing objects covered with a thin layer of snow and ice such as logs, rocks, stumps or numerous kinds of light brush. All will support enough snow to look firm but will fall through when sufficient weight is placed upon them. Also, in the spring, the sun warms rocks and other dark objects enough to melt all snow just below the surface, and when you are going from snow to rock you will find it is often easy to step through the thin lip.

Streams and Water Courses —
The best advice is to evaluate each situation individually. Water can undercut snow bridges and each crossing should be carefully checked. Logs or downed trees can sometimes be used but snow and ice make them more treacherous than normal. In planning a trip, consult maps beforehand to determine what water courses may lie in your path.

Drinking Water —
Getting water can be a serious problem for the winter traveller late in the winter when 8 to 12 feet of snow blankets the ground. Water must either be carried in with the party—an impossibility on multi-day trips—or some provision must be made for acquiring it. Small mountaineering stoves are commonly used for this purpose and an adequate fuel supply must be carried to ensure that melting capabilities will be equal to the needs of the party. Other methods may be employed in areas that have running water. The water is commonly visible—eight feet down under overhung banks, and just out of reach. Ingenuity is the only answer. A bucket and line is often suitable and can usually be rigged from gear in the party.

Tree-wells and tree-drip —
While not noticeable in early winter, tree-wells can become painfully obvious as winter progresses. Basically,

wells occur around tree trunks where branches keep snow from building up around the tree's base. Tree-wells are hazardous to ski over because they are often concrete-hard and icy. Or, with soft snow, a skier can take a fall next to one and become up-ended. When the temperature warms up, all snow on a tree falls off around it, creating tree-drip. When you ski downhill among the trees, tree-drip is a constant reality, and control on touring skis without steel edges can be tricky.

Wilderness Permits —
While the main emphasis is on individuals who use the wilderness areas during summer months, Forest Service officials indicate that permits to enter are now required year around.

The primary purpose of the permits is to chart the use each wilderness area receives. The permit system is not designed to check people in and out like a hotel register. They are available free at all ranger stations and at the supervisor's office for each national forest.

Winter Camping —
Camping is a natural part of ski touring. It extends touring from simple day outings to trips with larger goals and a multi-day setting. By simply spending the night out, you can accomplish much more in terms of acquiring a total winter experience.

The question of expanding your skill level to include winter camping is primarily one of equipment. What to take and how to use it are two topics well covered in numerous mountaineering and backpacking books.

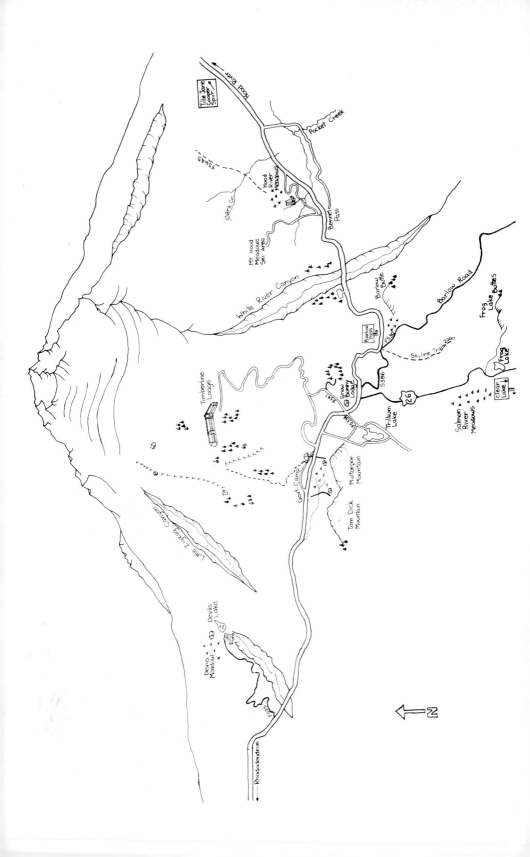

mt. hood tours

Mt. Hood, located a mere 50 miles east of Oregon's most populated district, is a prime drawing card for ski tourers in the Portland metropolitan area. It is a very accessible mountain.

Touring in close proximity to Mt. Hood is a many-sided experience. The mountain and its character dominate the scene. It is a temperamental mountain, given to unpredictable behavior and continually subjecting those who dally near its base to large doses of amazingly good and bad weather. When Hood is good, it is very, very good, and when it is bad, it is awful!

As experienced downhill skiers have come to find out, just because the skiing is bad at Government Camp or Timberline, does not always mean it is bad every place else. Consequently, when bad weather is encountered on the west side, head east. If it does not clear up near the junction of U.S. 26 and Oregon 35, head south. If you get down by Frog Lake or Clear Lake and it still is socked in, go to Bachelor.

Generally speaking, however, significantly better weather is found on the south and east sides of the mountain. The moist, wet clouds from the ocean seem to dump their loads to the west, and the snow is colder and drier on the east.

Ski tours on or near Mt. Hood embrace virtually all types of touring as it is practiced in Oregon. There are tours possible on roads, trails, lakes and the higher slopes above timberline. Some tours are in fairly close relationship with established downhill ski areas and might be appropriate for individuals who want to rent touring equipment and try the sport for several hours or an afternoon. Other tours are well removed from the whir and hum of the downhill scene and penetrate fully the silent world of the winter wilderness.

Touring in the Hood area can start early and last late, depending on the condition of the more permanent snowfields on the upper slopes of the mountain. Such tours would tend to relate closer to ski mountaineering or downhill skiing than to ski touring. Most tours are good from December or January to May, though those at lower elevations may have a shorter season.

Primary approach routes are via U.S. 26 from Portland to Government Camp or via Oregon 35 from Hood River. If you are going to tours on the east or north sides of the mountain, the Hood River approach, though longer, may save considerable time because of better conditions and lighter traffic.

devils meadow

Road and cross-country tour
4-6 miles round-trip
Mt. Hood National Forest
Zigzag Ranger District
Maps: Rhododendron and
   Government Camp Quadrangles

Devils Meadow is an open, marshy area at the lower end of a larger, sparsely-treed basin on the west side of Mt. Hood. It presents a destination with many possibilities. As with many sites located a considerable distance from main highways, the time of year and snow conditions determine the type of tour you will encounter.

In mid-winter, when heavy snows blanket the lower elevations and residents in nearby Rhododendron are shoveling their walks, the trip begins at the edge of U.S. 26. The distance to the meadow is 7 miles with an elevation gain of 1,800 feet. During the heavy snows of mid-winter, you can make a worthwhile tour of less distance, 4 miles one-way, to a significant viewpoint overlooking Devils Creek Falls and the upper Zigzag River valley.

In the spring as warm weather melts snow from lower elevations, the tour length shortens. Toward the end of the season with the opening of lower reaches of the road, the tour drops to a distance of 4 to 6 miles round-trip, the ideal length for an easy day's outing.

Once you reach the meadows, numerous possibilities are available. The road ends at Devils Meadow Forest Camp but the open floor of the basin permits touring up the drainage. Possible destinations include Devils Lake, two-thirds of a mile farther east, or the upper slopes of Zigzag Mountain for skiers who wish long downhill runs.

To get to Devils Meadow, drive on U.S. 26 to a point 1½ miles east of Rhododendron. Turn north on Forest Service Road 27. Follow FS27 for approximately one-half mile, then turn left at junction with FS27A. A sign reads: "Devils Meadow Campground 6½ Miles." Drive or ski on FS27 as far as snow level or ambition deems possible.

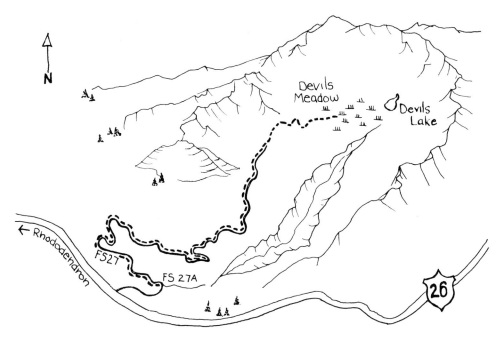

alpine ski trail

Trail tour
3½ miles one way (downhill)
Mt. Hood National Forest
Zigzag Ranger District
Map: Timberline Lodge Quadrangle

Alpine Ski Trail is located on the lower slopes of Mt. Hood and runs between Timberline Lodge and Government Camp. It is a trail for tourers with downhill abilities. Actually, the primary design of the trail was for downhill skiers who wanted a long run to Government Camp. In addition to the fact that it is well-marked with large signs every hundred yards, there are also several telephone stations along the route for emergency situations. The trail is patrolled only on the weekends.

Aside from these more citified aspects, the tour is enjoyable. The trail, 3½ miles in length, begins west of Timberline Lodge and ends at the Summit Ski Area at Government Camp—an elevation drop of 2,000 feet. Mt. Hood dominates the scene and the lesser peaks, plus Mt. Jefferson and Olallie Butte, spread out to the south.

While most people make the run in the traditional manner, starting at Timberline Lodge and skiing down, it is also possible to tour up from Government Camp, thus giving both an invigorating workout and eliminating the necessity of a car shuttle.

To make the tour, drive to Government Camp east of Portland on U.S. 26. If you want to ski up the trail, park at Summit Ski Area on the east end of Government Camp and simply ski uphill on the fringe of the area. The Alpine Ski Trail enters the area at the uppermost edge. The defile is plainly visible.

To begin at Timberline Lodge take the road to the lodge from Highway 26. Ski west past the lodge and continue through the chair lift area a short distance until a string of telephone lines and poles are visible, which head down the mountain. There are several signs posted in the area advising as to trails and conditions. The basic route is down a broad, open thoroughfare known as the Glade Ski Trail which continues to Government Camp. Approximately one-half mile below the lodge the Alpine Ski Trail veers off to the left. It is marked by a large orange sign.

Other touring possibilities exist in the vicinity on the same theme, i.e., a downhill run from Timberline to Government Camp. One is Forest Service Road S31 which begins below the lodge and services Phlox Point and Nanitch Campground. It lies between Apline Ski Trail and the Timberline Road. The other route is the previously mentioned Glade Trail, which is much on the order of Alpine Trail though somewhat longer and comes into Government Camp near the central business district.

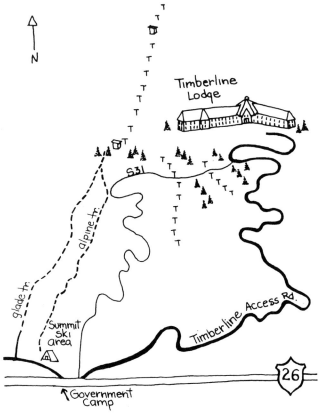

N

Timberline Lodge

S31

alpine tr.

glade tr.

Summit Ski area

Timberline Access Rd.

Government Camp

26

little zig zag

**Open country touring
2 miles round-trip
Mt. Hood National Forest
Zigzag Ranger District
Map: Timberline Lodge Quadrangle**

A ski tour to Little Zigzag Canyon is different. It embraces the world above timberline, the realm of the downhill skier or ski mountaineer, which is not to say that one world is better than another. It is simply to realize that there are distinctions.

The main difference between a ski tour and a ski mountaineering trip is the terrain and the condition of the snow found therein. Snow above timberline is subjected to the brunt of nature's forces. Windpack, ice, and deep powder all can be found above timberline, depending on local weather conditions. In many cases, the equipment used by tourers is somewhat inappropriate under icier conditions. Steel-edged skis with better edge-control offer more security and turning ability.

The above is not to say that skiing above timberline on touring skis and light bindings, is impossible. Many people, particularly those with past downhill experience, do an admirable job. Never-the-less, skiing the wide, fast, open slopes above the trees is a world apart from gliding the track on a frozen lakeshore.

Little Zigzag Canyon is more an example of what is possible above timberline than it is a hard and fast tour with a definite course and a fixed line of travel. Tour length is two miles, round-trip.

To reach Timberline Lodge drive to Government Camp on U.S. 26 east of Portland. Timberline Lodge is 7 miles from U.S. 26 via plowed access road. There is ample parking.

From the lodge, head northwest, cross under chairlifts and contour around the mountain while you gradually pick up altitude. The trees are sparse near the lodge and eventually vanish. The gorge which is Little Zigzag Canyon soon becomes evident as you proceed west. Farther west Zigzag Canyon below Zigzag Glacier and Mississippi Head also become visible.

You should take care when approaching Little Zigzag Canyon because of windblown cornices which make canyon rims treacherous. Weather is also another potential matter of concern above timberline. While landmarks are evident and tracks distinguishable in the sun and beauty of a crisp spring day, weather changes fast in the mountains and in a few hours conditions can switch to total whiteout. The prudent tourer keeps one eye skyward at all times.

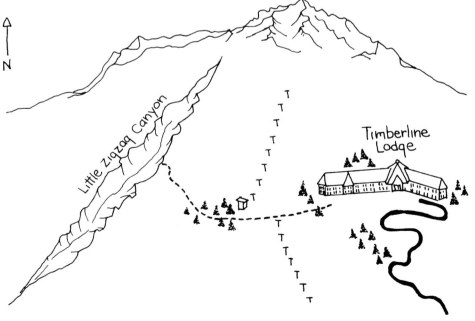

Little Zigzag Canyon

N

Timberline Lodge

21

multorpor meadows

Road tour plus cross-country option
3 miles round-trip
Mt. Hood National Forest
Zigzag Ranger District
Maps: Government Camp Quadrangle or Mt. Hood Wilderness
   (free from Forest Service)

Multorpor Meadows, located directly across U.S. 26 from Government Camp between Multorpor and Ski Bowl downhill areas, is an ideal touring site for anyone attempting touring for the first time. It is also convenient for groups of mixed skiers, both downhill and cross-country, who may be enjoying alpine skiing at a number of nearby areas.

Touring at Multorpor offers a number of possibilities. A simple option is some easy touring amid meadows and ponds within sight of Multorpor ski area's parking lot.

A second option is a number of formal cross-country trails traversing the meadows which are flagged at various times during the winter for Nordic racing events. Information on the location and condition of these trails should be available at the downhill ski areas.

The third alternative involves a combination of the first two. The tour begins from the edge of the parking lot adjacent to the rope tow at Multorpor. The route skirts the lower edge of the ski area, heads west, and parallels the Multorpor chair lift for 100 yards before veering to the right on a snowed-in summer access road leading to Ski Bowl.

The road, plainly visible, is wide, rolling and easily followed. It eventually intersects the open slopes of Ski Bowl where another road, broader and minus the rolling features of the first, swings abruptly north. Follow it to where it crosses a small stream, Camp Creek.

At Camp Creek there are again three choices: 1.) Continue skiing north on the road and emerge on U.S. 26. Walk or hitchhike back to the parking area; 2.) Retrace the track already created; 3.) Cross either of the forks of Camp Creek then ski east. A footbridge connects the two forks which come together upstream at the road's base to a finger of land. By staying between the creeks, you will eventually emerge at the meadows, a short distance from the parking lot.

For the experienced tourer, option No. 3 is a pleasant trip. For the less experienced, however, it should be noted that the elevation lost on the easy glide down to Camp Creek is now picked up among the trees, and a circuitous route around unyielding obstacles can sometimes try a neophyte's patience. Once you reach the meadows it all becomes worthwhile.

To reach Multorpor Meadows, drive to Government Camp on Highway 26 some 60 miles east of Portland and follow the signs to the ski area. Starting point for all three options is the rope tow adjacent to the parking lot. The meadows lie to the northwest. While most areas around Mt. Hood are Forest Service land and, hence, open to the public, the meadows are actually owned privately. Tourers and other non-motorized users are welcome as long as they interact with the environment in a positive manner.

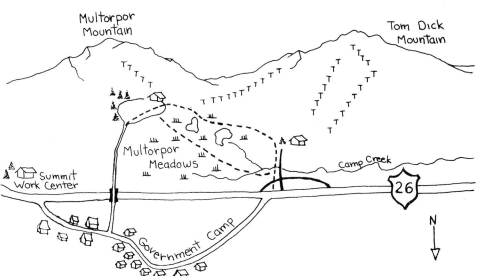

Multorpor
Mountain

Tom Dick
Mountain

Summit
Work Center

Multorpor
Meadows

Camp Creek

26

Government Camp

N

trillium lake

**Road tour plus cross-country
3 miles round-trip
Mt. Hood National Forest
Zigzag Ranger District
Map: Timberline Lodge Quadrangle**

Trillium Lake offers a mixed bag: it begins as a road tour, switches to a cross-country ramble along snow-covered waterways and marshes and ends with a lake tour and a striking view of Mt. Hood. In mid-winter with good snow, firm ice and a taste of sunshine, it is a guaranteed turn-on for even the most stodgy downhiller.

Trillium Lake Basin lies almost due south of Mt. Hood, 4½ air miles from Timberline Lodge. Parking is ample

and available, plus easy to find. To begin, drive on U.S Highway 26 to Government Camp, 60 miles east of Portland, then continue east for 2 miles more on U.S. 26 until you arrive at Snow Bunny Lodge, a snow play area closed to skiing. Park in the parking lot. The tour to Trillium Lake begins directly across the highway.

Snowmobiles use the parking area and trails in the vicinity of the lake but you only share a brief one-half mile with them before the route leaves the beaten path and wends its way into more pleasing territory.

From the junction of U.S. 26 and Forest Service Road 334, ski down a gentle hill until the road flattens out and enters a broad, open meadow at the one-half mile mark. A powerline runs through the meadow. From the road's inter-

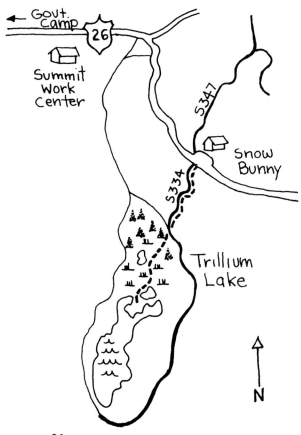

section with the meadow, snowmobile routes go left and right. The tour goes directly across the meadow to a fringe of small trees and enters larger trees on the clearing's far side. Ski in as straight a line as possible, bearing to the left or south, if any deviation is to be made at all. Openings should be visible a short distance into the trees and soon you should emerge on the edge of the marshes and snow-covered waterways, which eventually lead to Trillium Lake. Merely follow the meandering creek—open country touring —and arrive at the lake.

Because of its rather low elevation (3,601 feet), Trillium Lake should be carefully inspected for thin ice before you venture out upon it. If conditions are suspect, follow the shoreline to the southern end of the lake for a view of Mt. Hood 7 miles to the north.

snow bunny

Road tour
3½ miles round-trip
Mt. Hood National Forest
Zigzag Ranger District
Map: Timberline Lodge Quadrangle

This is a secret tour. It has been lurking behind the Snow Bunny Lodge snow play area for a long time, and few people have really appreciated it. They drive on by or get in a big hassle with snowmobilers when they both try to use the road to Trillium Lake across the highway.

Signs around the Snow Bunny Lodge may indicate no skiing, but they refer to downhill skiing, and if you carry your gear across the property to the beginning of Forest Service Road S347, there should be no problem. To find exactly where the road begins, follow a series of lighting poles north past the lodge. The roadway becomes obvious.

Tour length is 3½ miles round-trip. The road parallels the West Fork of the Salmon River for over a mile and eventually crosses it shortly beyond the junction with road FS347A. At this junction, FS347 continues to the right another two-thirds of a mile and finally ends in a clearcut harvest area. The left fork, FS347A, goes north one-half mile and intersects the Timberline Lodge access road 1½ miles from U.S. 26.

As with most tours, possibilities for the trip are many. The road climbs all the way from Snow Bunny. The fork to the Timberline road continues climbing while the one to the clearcut levels out, prior to a last short hill before the unit. In either instance under good conditions with an adequate track, the run back to Snow Bunny has enough grade to allow easy sliding.

Snow Bunny Lodge is located 2 miles east of Government Camp on U.S. Highway 26, a mile from the junction of U.S. 26 and Oregon 35. A large parking lot is shared by hill sliders, ski tourers and snowmobilers and the route to Snow Bunny Lodge is well-marked.

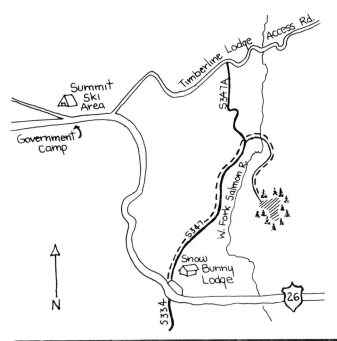

barlow pass

Road and trail tour
1-4 miles round-trip
Mt. Hood National Forest
Bear Springs Ranger District
Map: Timberline Lodge Quadrangle

Ski touring down the Old Barlow Road can be a pioneering experience. If you have never been there before, don't have an accurate map and try to figure things out with seven feet of snow on the ground, chances are you will really begin to wonder how the pioneers actually made it through there in the first place.

After much pondering, two trips to the area and a close check of three maps, it suddenly becomes apparent that a major change has taken place on Oregon 35 and that the highway has been relocated cutting off a curve and creating a scenic byway. Few recent maps record this fact. The resulting confusion re-emphasizes the need to maintain an up-to-date map file and, more importantly, how easy it is to get misled in an unfamiliar snowed-in environment.

Once you understand the lay of the land near Barlow Pass, three touring options quickly become evident. All begin at the parking area on the south side of Oregon 35 opposite a sign pointing to Barlow Road.

The first and most popular run follows the historic Barlow Wagon Road south from the pass to an open meadow at the base of Barlow Butte, 1¼ miles and 437 feet below Oregon 35. Devils Half

Acre Meadow Campground is nearby and north of the site of the former Barlow Guard Station. To reach the meadows, ski on the road leading south from the parking area on Oregon 35. This is actually the cut-off portion of the old highway, and in late spring a sign protrudes from the snow and proclaims Barlow Pass to be several hundred yards south of its current location on Oregon 35. It also claims to be 2 feet higher.

Ski south on the old highway for 200 yards, then turn left and downhill on the Old Barlow Road, now designated Forest Service S30. The road drops pleasantly for 1 mile and winds among young trees and occasional stands of large firs. It is a road of a former era, in tune with the forest and lacking the need to inflict itself on the environment as a gravel and concrete monument to engineering.

The second option is the Pacific Crest Trail, No. 2000 (Oregon Skyline Trail), which joins the old highway a short distance beyond the Barlow Road junction on the left side of the roadway. The Skyline Trail in this area is trail skiing at its best. Straightaways, curves and bumps caused by tree-wells all offer a fair challenge for the skier who prefers this style of touring. As winter progresses, the trail, generally well-defined, may become difficult to follow when blazes and pruned limbs vanish as the snow depth increases.

The third and final option is simply to follow the old highway, now a scenic loop known as Forest Service Road S386, for as far as desire takes you. The highway, which is wider and flatter than the Barlow Road, drops at a gentle rate and provides a suitable practice run for beginners.

Barlow Pass is 6 miles east of Government Camp on Oregon 35. To reach it, drive east of Portland on U.S. 26 past Government Camp to the junction of 26 and Oregon 35. From this junction travel east on 35 for 2½ miles to the pass. Parking for several vehicles is usually available on the south side of the highway.

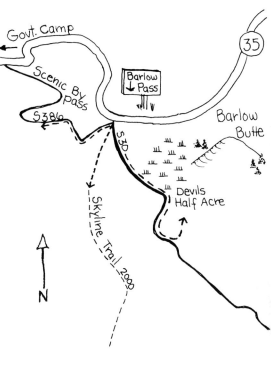

white river canyon

Open country touring
4 miles round-trip
Mt. Hood National Forest
Zigzag Ranger District
Map: Mt. Hood Wilderness
    (free from the Forest Service)

The White River Canyon, an open flat-land gently ascending to the steeper flanks of Mt. Hood, is described by former Forest Ranger Dick Buscher as perhaps THE premium tour on the Zigzag Ranger District.

The primary appeal of the tour is easy access. Turnouts near the White River Bridge on Oregon 35 are plowed out between storms and an off-highway parking lot slightly west of the bridge on the road's north side is also kept open.

The tour is excellent for the beginner. On clear days Mt. Hood is radiant, a constant companion. Tour length is variable depending on the desires of the party. Beyond the 2 mile mark, however, the terrain steepens, and a lack of trees and other vegetation often leads to icier conditions than are found below timberline.

Because of the changing course of the White River, you should exercise caution in picking a route up the stream bed. While the canyon floor is several hundred yards across, the meandering course often brings it close to cut-banks on one side or another, and, if you are touring on the cut-bank side, avalanches from cornices can be a danger. In recent years, the best route has been on the east side of the river. Additional care should be taken concerning river crossings on snow bridges and during any approach to the river bank, which tends to be undercut.

White River Canyon is 4½ miles east of the junction of U.S. 26 and Oregon 35, east of Government Camp. Once you reach the White River Bridge, you can begin touring immediately on the north side of the highway.

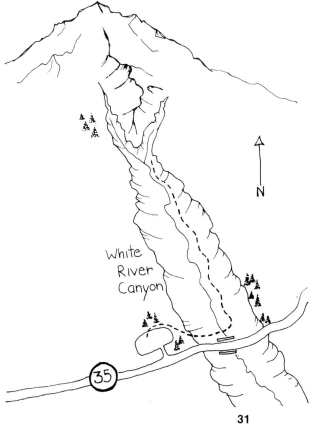

White
River
Canyon

N

35

hood river meadows

**Road tour
4 miles round-trip
Mt. Hood National Forest
Hood River Ranger District
Map: Timberline Quadrangle**

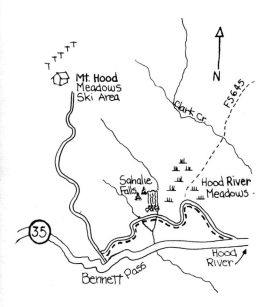

Ski tourers desiring a maximum return from a minimum of invested time would do well to visit Hood River Meadows. The basic route for the tour is an old section of Oregon 35 which was made into a scenic bypass when the road was straightened, just north of Bennett Pass on the southeast side of Mt. Hood.

For new skiers, the best approach to the meadows is made by beginning the tour at the higher Bennett Pass starting point. A shuttle vehicle can be left at the lower end where the scenic route rejoins Oregon 35, slightly more than 1 mile north of Bennett Pass on the left side of the highway. Other route options are available to people who want longer or shorter tours.

In addition to the meadows, which are cut by Meadows Creek and provide good views of Mt. Hood, another scenic attraction is Sahalie Falls on the East Fork of the Hood River. It is situated on the scenic loop midway between Hood River Meadows and Bennett Pass.

The tour, 2 miles in length from entry to exit, offers neophytes a chance to try their skills with a minimum of uphill skiing and with plenty of visual remuneration. Sites for overnight camping are found near the meadows and a number of trails exist for exploration, notably Trail 645 which departs near Hood River Meadows Forest Camp and heads north in the direction of Clark Creek.

To get to Hood River Meadows, drive east of Government Camp on U.S. 26 and take Oregon 35 to Bennett Pass.

Another alternative is to approach from Hood River on Oregon 35. Follow the signs to the turn-off to Hood River Meadows Ski Area.

The road to the meadows intersects the ski area access road a short distance west of Bennett Pass. Parking usually is available close by unless recent snows have clogged road shoulders.

pocket creek

Road tour
8 miles round-trip
Mt. Hood National Forest
Hood Ranger District
Map: Badger Lake Quadrangle

A ski tour to Pocket Creek is a many-splendored journey. You begin with some flats. Cross a river on a bridge. Trudge up a hillside. Snake through the forest. And eventually, winding around a corner, you cross the threshold into a vast opening, traverse its wideness and . . . suddenly . . . meet Mt. Hood face on.

Pocket Creek is a small mountain stream draining into the East Fork of the Hood River, east of Bennett Pass and south of Oregon 35. It is a good tour for skiers of many skill levels because it offers a basically simple roadway for primary and uncomplicated travel, plus numerous side-trips and enticing open slopes with long runs available to those who seek them.

Essentially the scene is a logging road with a number of clearcut harvest areas. While several clearcuts exist within 2 miles of the trailhead, the best units begin at the 3 mile mark, where the Pocket Creek basin intersects the East Fork drainage.

At Pocket Creek, there is a choice of route. One road, paralleling Pocket Creek, goes south and up, circles the entirety of the Pocket Creek basin and ends in a large clearcut.

The second route, the approach road, continues west, not gaining much altitude, and parallels the East Fork, eventually ending in a clearcut less than 1 mile from Bennett Pass. Again there are some choices: 1.) Return to the trailhead via the existing track; 2.) Go cross-country to Bennett Pass and wait for a shuttle vehicle. 3.) Go cross-country to Bennett Pass, then loop back to the cars on the road shoulder which parallels Oregon 35.

Starting point for the tour is the junction of Oregon 35 and Forest Service Road S300, located 30 miles south of Hood River on Oregon 35. S300 begins 1 mile south of the Robin Hood Campground on the left side of the highway. A sign pointing east reads: "East Fork Hood River—1 mile, Pocket Creek—3 miles." Follow this road.

If you are approaching from the west via Government Camp, follow Oregon 35 to Bennett Pass and the turn-off to Mt. Hood Meadows Ski Area. The road to Pocket Creek is 3.3 miles north of this junction.

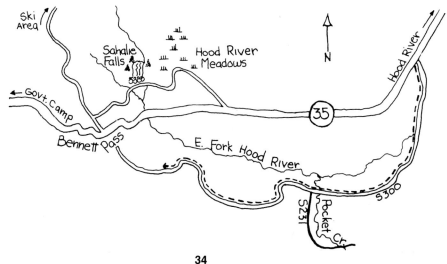

cooper spur - tilly jane

Trail tour
6 miles round-trip
Mt. Hood National Forest
Hood River Ranger District
Map: Dog River and Cathedral Ridge Quadrangles and Mt. Hood Wilderness
  (free from the Forest Service)

The Cooper Spur Ski Trail is a challenging 3 mile ski tour from Cooper Spur Ski Area to Tilly Jane Campground. If offers variety for those who wish a winter interlude in a seldom-visited environment.

The trail is steep. Elevation gain in 3 miles is 1,500 feet. It is not a tour for anyone lacking downhill technique, particularly early in the year when rocks and stumps threaten the unwary.

For overnight outings the Tilly Jane Campground offers a number of choices: two Forest Service shelters exist, both open, and one is perhaps the most elaborate shelter yet remaining in the Oregon Cascades—a veritable Viking longhouse.

That shelter, approximately 40 feet long and two storied, features a sleeping loft, indoor toilets, a circular fireplace and a wood stove. A second smaller shelter is adjacent and several other outbuildings are nearby. The campground, reached in summer by the Cloud Cap Road (the long way to get there) is completely isolated once the snows of winter commence.

A third possibility for shelter is the former Tilly Jane Guard Station, now leased to a Hood River climbing organization, the Alpinees. Use of this structure is possible on a fee basis. Information on the cabin is available from the operators of the Cooper Spur Ski Area.

To get to Cooper Spur, drive to the northeast side of Mt. Hood via Oregon 35 from Hood River or by U.S. 26 from Portland. The turn-off to Cooper Spur is on Oregon 35 near Polallie Campground, 10 miles north of the turn-off to Hood River Meadows Ski Area. Cooper Spur facilities are located on a loop of Forest Service Road S12, and the route in from Oregon 35 is well-signed.

Once at the ski area you will find the Cooper Spur Ski Trail by traversing the primary slope to the half-way point where a road bisects the hill and enters the timber on the west side of the area. Follow the road one-quarter mile into the timber until it doubles back. The trail departs from the switchback. It is 3 miles to Tilly Jane.

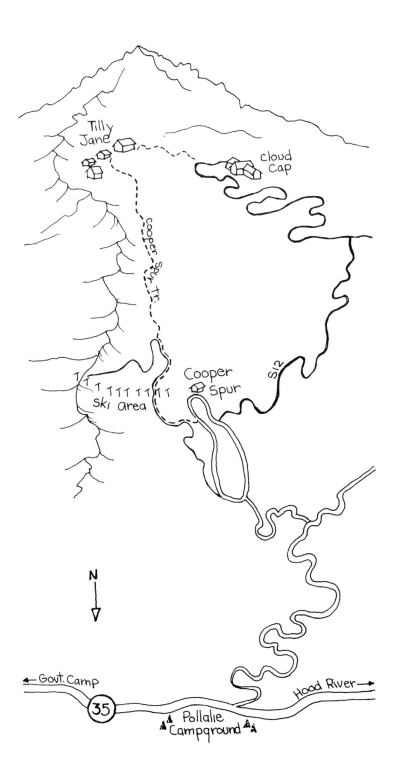

Tilly Jane

Cloud Cap

Cooper Spur Tr.

Cooper Spur

Ski Area

S12

N

←Govt. Camp

35

Hood River→

Pollalie Campground

salmon river meadows

Road tour
3 miles round-trip
Mt. Hood National Forest
Bear Springs Ranger District
Map: Mt. Wilson Quadrangle

Finding Salmon River Meadows is tricky. In reward for trickiness the persevering will find a touring experience unique to the vicinity. No snowmobiles enter the area. Coyote tracks dot the meadows. In the spring, birds sing and wheel overhead, and the meadows, marshy as the snow recedes, awake to the coming of a new season.

In short, it is a step apart from the roar of the highway which is audible in the distance. As with wilderness areas in the more classical sense, man is only a visitor who does not remain. Mt. Hood, ever present to the north, surveys the scene—the eternal watchman.

Salmon River Meadows lies south of Mt. Hood, 5¾ miles east of Government Camp. Drive east of Government Camp to the junction of U.S. 26 and Oregon 35. Turn south on U.S. 26 and proceed a little more than 2 miles to a prominent Union 76 gas station. The access road to the meadows intersects U.S. 26 four-tenths of a mile south of the station. The road, west and below U.S. 26, is narrow and somewhat overgrown and is marked by a sign: "S400, Dead End Road." There is no immediate parking and the junction of S400 with U.S. 26 is very indistinct. The nearest parking is a widened shoulder further to the south.

The road to the meadows, less than 1 mile in length, drops gradually and is a pleasant ski, though fallen timber and a number of streams may make some detours necessary.

As the road bottoms out, the meadows become visible beyond the screen of trees. Access is easy unless receding

spring snowbanks create temporary marshes around the meadows.

Once you gain the meadows your direction is dictated only by the snow consistency and the desires of the party. The main meadow is perhaps 1¼ miles long, and several additional small marsh areas appear along Salmon River as it flows on south.

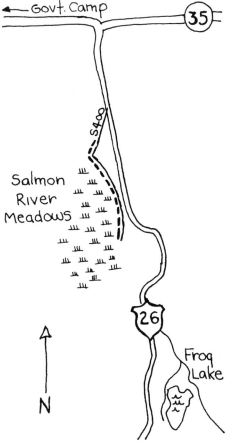

frog lake buttes

Road tour
6 miles round-trip
Mt. Hood National Forest
Bear Springs Ranger District
Map: Mt. Wilson Quadrangle

Let's say you are from Portland and you want to go ski touring. "Go to Government Camp," people say, "there is good touring up there."

Arrive Government Camp. Rain.

A hopeless day?

Try Frog Lake Buttes.

The Buttes, located a significant distance southeast of Mt. Hood and the weather systems which seem to hover in the Government Camp-Timberline Area, are an alternative to the wet rain all too often found on the west side of the mountain.

The tour to the top of Frog Lake Buttes is a road tour; however, because of an elevation gain of 1,400 feet and a narrow path at high elevation caused by increased snow depth, the downhill run can be challenging.

A significant factor in determining just the amount of challenge involved depends on the time of year you attempt it and the weather conditions. It also depends upon the snowmobile traffic.

Departure point for the tour is a parking lot plowed throughout the winter and used during its duration by snowmobilers who travel a series of trails marked and laid out for them by the Mt. Hood National Forest. While the trip up Frog Lake Buttes is included as a potential snowmobile route, few machines seem to venture more than a mile up the road because of its narrow character and a problem with windfalls which hinder progress. In late spring, lower portions of the tour are rutted and washboard-like and good route picking on the way up can avoid the icier dips on the way down.

From the junction of U.S. 26 and Oregon 35, travel south on U.S 26 for 4¼ miles to the Frog Lake junction. This junction is plowed out and a large parking lot is located on the east side of the highway. The trail to Frog Lake Buttes starts on the south side of the parking lot.

Tour length is somewhat uncertain. A road sign at the junction says 3 miles while a Forest Service brochure says 2½. Estimate: between 5 and 6 miles round-trip.

To start the tour, sign in at a Forest Service winter registration box adjacent to the trail near the edge of the parking lot. User statistics are valuable in determining which areas get certain status —an important factor in the growing conflict between the motorized and the more purist user groups.

From the registration box, follow the road one-quarter mile south to its junction with S458H, the road to Frog Lake Buttes. It is also designated via signs as snowmobile trail "A."

While lower sections of the trail are used by snowmobilers, the traffic seems to reduce substantially beyond a large clearcut one-half mile up the road. The route heads to the southeast until the last one-half mile, then turns abruptly northeast, follows the ridge and moves through open meadows with tree-lined fringes as you approach the top. Views of Mt. Hood, Mt. Jefferson and White River Canyon are possible from the summit.

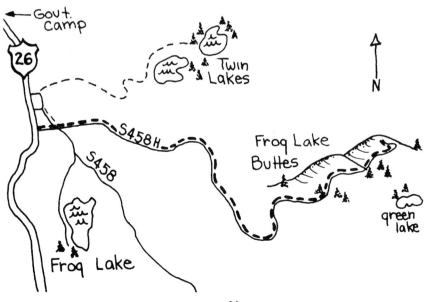

frog lake

Road tour
1½ miles round-trip
Mt. Hood National Forest
Bear Springs Ranger District
Map: Mt. Wilson Quadrangle

A ski tour to Frog Lake is a trip of short duration. Round-trip distance is not more than 1½ miles, less if you leave the main road and cut down through the trees to the lakeshore.

The trip is an easy road tour suited to first-time skiers or to family groups desiring an afternoon ski with the small fry. As with a number of the more popular ski tours in the Mt. Hood vicinity, the Frog Lake tour is also a popular jaunt for snowmobilers and has been publicized as such by the Mt. Hood National Forest. Most snowmobile trails in the region are longer, and while some machines do travel to the lake, most seem intent on going beyond to other points. Travel during the week and early and late in the season should assure minimum contact, though late season trips do find roadways in a washboard-like condition. This can be a nuisance to new skiers attempting to keep their balance in an unfamiliar environment.

Frog Lake lies southeast of Mt. Hood along U.S. 26, 7¼ miles southeast of Government Camp. Drive east of Government Camp 3 miles to the junction of U.S. 26 and Oregon 35. Turning south on 26, you travel 4½ miles to the Frog Lake junction which is well-signed. A large parking lot is located on the east side of the junction.

From the parking area, the lake lies three-quarters of a mile to the south. Forest Service Road S458 leaves the parking area and travels southeast. You will encounter two junctions. At the first, a four-way intersection, continue straight ahead. At the second, take the right-hand or southwest fork which skirts and parallels the lake for some distance, but eventually reaches Frog Lake Campground. Ample signs in the area should reduce confusion.

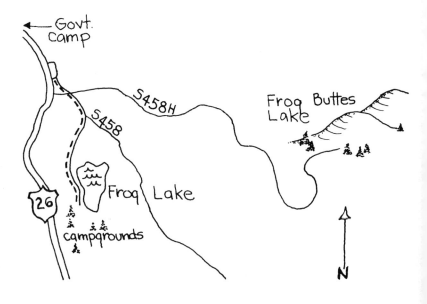

clear lake butte

Road tour
6-12 miles round-trip
Mt. Hood National Forest
Bear Springs Ranger District
Map: Mt. Wilson Quadrangle

Clear Lake Butte has its own personality. Unlike many tours in the shadow of Mt. Hood, the Butte is not dominated by the glowering image of the loftier mountain. Rather, Hood is a nice vista on the horizon, merely one pleasant aspect of a totally pleasing scene.

Access to Clear Lake Butte comes from the famed Skyline Road, Forest Service Road S42, which follows the crest of the Cascades in the southern portion of the Mt. Hood National Forest.

To reach Skyline Road, drive to its junction with U.S. 26 8¾ miles south of the junction of U.S. 26 and Oregon 35. Follow Skyline Road 3 miles to its intersection with S405. This is the road to the top of Clear Lake Butte.

Depending on the season, it may or may not be possible to drive from the junction of U.S. 26 and the Skyline Road to S405. Drive as far as possible. S405 begins as a medium-standard route and then deteriorates and steepens

as the tour progresses. From its junction with the Skyline Road, S405 runs north for three-quarters of a mile, passes a clearcut and then turns sharply west. Another road continues north but if there is any question as to the correct route, simply follow the telephone line which leads to the lookout station on the summit. It parallels the road most of the way. According to signs, it is 3 miles to the lookout from the junction of Skyline Road and S405 and is an elevation gain of 880 feet.

If you visit Clear Lake Butte late in the touring season, chances are fair that snow may be a little sparse around the summit lookout tower. The top portion of the butte has been logged to afford a good view for the lookout and the sun's rays are freer to do their work than along the forested road at lower elevation.

From the lookout, Mt. Hood is large but not overpowering and Clear Lake and Timothy Lake to the north and southwest spread out below in a world of white.

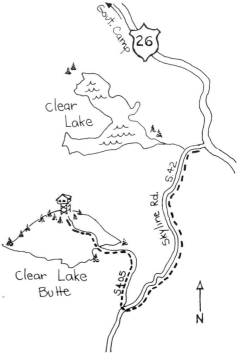

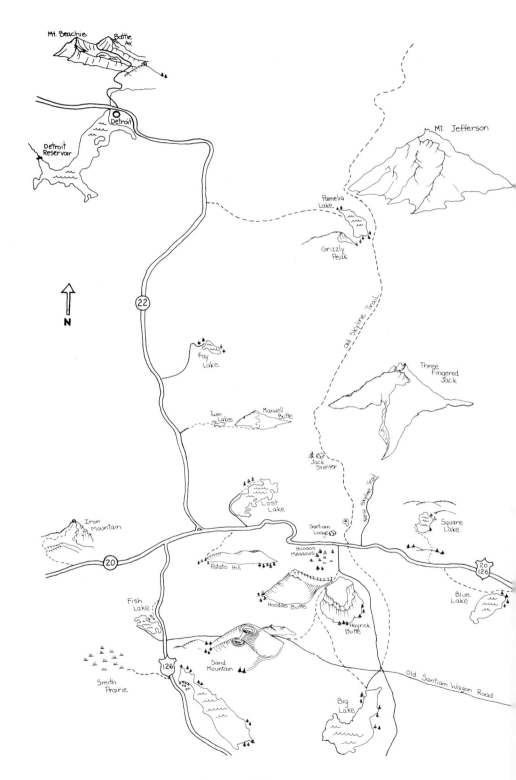

Mt. Beachie
Battle Ax
Detroit
Detroit Reservoir
MT. JEFFERSON
Pamelia Lake
Grizzly Peak
Old Skyline Trail
22
N
Fay Lake
Three Fingered Jack
Twin Lakes
Maxwell Butte
Jack Shelter
Lost Lake
New Skyline Trail
Santiam Lodge
Square Lake
Iron Mountain
Hoodoo Meadows
20
Potato Hill
Hoodoo Butte
20 126
Blue Lake
Fish Lake
Haynick Butte
126
Sand Mountain
Old Santiam Wagon Road
Smith Prairie
Big Lake

santiam pass & northern willamette national forest

The ski tours described in this section represent a broad range of touring possibilities centered primarily on the highways approaching Santiam Pass from the west and east. The highways, Oregon 22, U.S. 20 and U.S. 126 serve primarily the northern, central and southern sectors of the Willamette Valley and continue east to Central Oregon as U.S. 20 after their merger near Santiam Pass.

For ease in location, tours are listed in geographic order from Elk Lake in the north to Clear Lake in the south. Each tour has one or more approaches, depending from which locality the tourer is coming.

All tours in this section are in the Willamette or Deschutes National Forests. You may obtain up-to-date maps of the areas from the Forest Service ranger stations located at Detroit, Sweet Home, McKenzie Bridge or Sisters. Once you gain some familiarity with the region, further touring possibilities should become obvious.

In addition to the skiing offered by these routes there are other attractions. Five of the tours are within the boundaries of the Mt. Jefferson Wilderness Area. On clear days, Mt. Jefferson, Mt. Washington, Three Fingered Jack and the Three Sisters often can be seen from vantage points.

As has been explained previously, in attempting to describe ski tours, a question which often arises is one of difficulty. Depending on the user-group and experience, some tours are more appropriate than others. The following generalizations are therefore made:

I. Tours suitable for neophytes: Road Tours
Big Lake/Hoodoo
Clear Lake
Elk Lake
Fay Lake
Fish Lake
Hoodoo Meadows
Lost Lake
Potato Hill
Smith Prairie

II. Tours for experienced skiers: Trail skiing and/or more complex tours
Blue Lake Trail
Iron Mountain
Jack Shelter
New Skyline Trail
Pamelia Lake
San Mountain Traverse
Square Lake
Maxwell Butte/Twin Lakes Trail

A number of tours—notably those to Jack Shelter, Fay Lake, Square Lake, Elk Lake, Pamelia Lake and Twin Lakes —offer good destinations for overnight outings. Once you reach the major objectives, tours to nearby attractions are always available.

Finally, extended, long-distance trips are possible. Once you understand the basic geography of several adjacent areas, you can forge new routes. An example would be a Jack Shelter-to-Twin Lakes traverse, starting at Santiam Pass and ending at the bottom of the Maxwell Butte Trail on Oregon 22. In short, the options are endless; take these trails as but a mere introduction and innovate from there.

elk lake

Road tour
6-9 miles round-trip
Mt. Hood/Willamette National Forests
Detroit Ranger District
Map: Battle Ax Quadrangle

Elk Lake lies in a small basin at the foot of Battle Ax Mountain 15 miles from Detroit Reservoir on the southern-most boundary of the Mt. Hood National Forest.

A prime element in the desirability of the Elk Lake region is easy access to good snow. Because of the lake's location, deep in a shaded valley between two peaks, snow is skiable long into the spring.

A high standard Forest Service road, S46, leaves the community of Detroit on the east end of Detroit Reservoir and follows the Breitenbush River for 6 miles to a fork. Take the left fork, road S80, which continues for three-quarters of a mile to another junction. Again, take the left fork paralleling Humbug Creek and continue for 3¼ miles. At approximately 3 miles S80 takes a hard right turn. It is beyond this junction that the gain in altitude begins. In 1½ miles the road climbs nearly one thousand feet (from BM 2760' to BM 3748' at Dunlap Saddle). Drive as far up as possible.

In the spring, depending upon snow fall and a predominent southern exposure, the road is often bare virtually to the saddle where parking for several cars is usually available. From the saddle an easy 2 mile road tour over rolling terrain brings the skier to the east end of Elk Lake and a bridge over Elk Creek. Follow the road another three-quarters of a mile, uphill on the north side of the lake; then, drop down via the road on the west end of the lake to an open meadow and campsites.

For a longer tour (this whole trip is an excellent overnight tour for a beginner since the ski-in with a large pack is short and not difficult), return to the main road above the lake and continue west and upward another 1½ miles to Beachie Saddle. From this point on clear days Mt. Jefferson is visible to the southeast and Battle Ax Creek and valley spread out west of the divide.

For a more stunning view of the surrounding country, climb Battle Ax Mountain. A trail to the top takes off directly from Beachie Saddle. Because of the steepness and the rockiness of the terrain, skis should be left at the saddle, but poles are handy and a real aid in the ascent. The trail can be followed in numerous switchbacks up the southwest slope of the mountain, but for the last mile it will be lost in deep snow.

Do not venture too far to the western side of the mountain as steep slopes of wind-packed snow and iced-rock make unroped-going hazardous. Exercise caution on the summit as wind-built cornices project far beyond the edges of base-rock drop-offs. From the top, major summits from Mt. Rainier to Diamond Peak are visible during good weather.

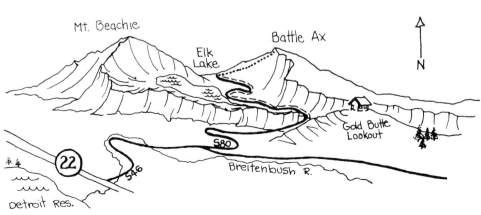

Mt. Beachie

Battle Ax

Elk Lake

N

Gold Butte Lookout

S80

22

546

Breitenbush R.

Detroit Res.

pamelia lake

Road and trail tour
8-12 miles round-trip
Willamette National Forest
Detroit Ranger District
Map: Mt. Jefferson Wilderness Area
**   (free from U.S. Forest Service)**

Ski touring to Pamelia Lake is a classic example of the "Imprecise Tour." The variables of season, weather and snow level effectively regulate its duration. The shortest possible round-trip distance for the tour is 4 miles. The longest is 12½ miles. Snow level, forever fluctuating, is the final distance-maker.

Whatever the distance, the tour to Pamelia Lake is worthwhile, and during the spring months the round-trip usually is 6 to 8 miles.

To reach Pamelia Lake, drive east of Salem on Oregon 22 past Detroit Reservoir to the community of Idanha. From Idanha continue southeast on Oregon 22 for 8 miles to the intersection of the Pamelia Lake Road, FS109. It is 4¼ miles east on FS109 to Pamelia Lake trailhead and an additional 2 miles by trail to the lake. Elevation at the junction of FS109 and Oregon 22 is 2300′ whereas the elevation at Pamelia Lake is 3884′. Drive as far as possible on FS109; then begin skiing. Basically, the road is a gradual uphill climb; however, there is one short downhill section about a mile prior to the trailhead.

Once on the actual trail, you will find the tour is thoroughly enjoyable. It parallels Pamelia Creek the entire distance to the lake and winds through a stand of some of the largest fir yet remaining on the west slope of the Cascades.

The trail, a lazy glide coming out, will have few tight corners or drops if care is taken setting the track on the way in.

If the ice is firm on the lake, you can ski toward the base of Grizzly Peak on the southern shore with stunning views of Mt. Jefferson almost directly above to the northeast.

Note: the lake is reported to be open year-around to fishing, with a limit of 30 fish per day and no minimum length limit. However, this information should be checked annually in the Game Commission regulations. Anyone planning to fish the lake during the winter should carry an axe or shovel to break a hole through the ice layers. Be sure to check the ice carefully before venturing on it in the spring.

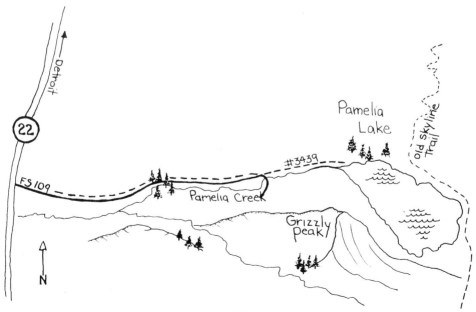

fay lake

Road tour
6 miles round-trip
Willamette National Forest
Detroit Ranger District
Map: Mt. Jefferson Wilderness Area (free from the U.S. Forest Service)

A 3-mile road tour, offering the dips and climbs of a regular trail but no tree-wells or tight corners, brings the winter adventurer to Fay Lake, a small body of ice-covered water slightly west of the Mt. Jefferson Wilderness Area.

The trail to Fay Lake has a charm all its own. There is no majestic view of snow-capped mountains on the far horizon, but there is a close look at the things which make a wilderness experience unique: large trees, and the rush and tumble of the North Santiam River amid six-foot snow banks. There is easy sliding on the track back out with gentle runs through a dripping forest.

The road to Fay Lake is not a typical Forest Service "super highway." It is well over-hung with trees, and on warm days the tourer is pelted by descending droplets or an occasional clump of snow. Tree-drip and the resulting icy patches lend excitement to assorted downhill runs, but the trail is neither difficult nor hard to follow.

Take U.S. 20 or U.S. 126 from the Willamette Valley to the junction with Oregon 22 at the Santiam "Y," a few miles west of the summit of Santiam Pass. At this junction follow Oregon 22 northwest as if headed for Salem, for 6 miles. At this point you will arrive at the junction of two roads, FS1349E on the west side of Oregon 22 and FS110 on the east side. A sign, if visible, should point east to Big Meadows. Ski east on FS110.

The tour begins with a slight downhill run from the roadside, then progresses for the first 1½ miles with a fairly even number of ups and downs until you reach a bridge crossing the North San-

tiam. From this point it is a gradual climb with several level spots for the remaining distance to Fay Lake. After sufficient snowfall and cold weather, it is safe to ski on the lake, but early in the year or during warming periods you should be careful. Generally, skis spread out the body weight and tourers should avoid walking on the lake without them.

Note: a new, wide Forest Service logging road bisects FS110 one mile from the starting point. Merely cross it and continue down the much narrower defile which is unmistakably FS110 and of much older origin.

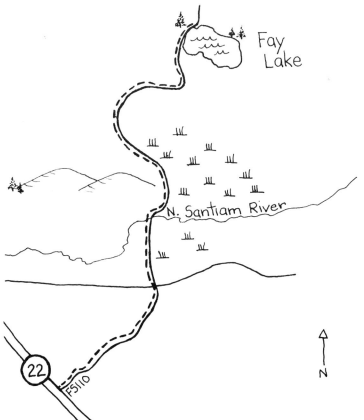

Fay
Lake

N. Santiam River

22
FS1110

N

maxwell butte

Trail tour
6-8 miles round trip
Willamette National Forest
Detroit Ranger District
Map: Mt. Jefferson Wilderness Area (free from U.S. Forest Service)

The Maxwell Butte Trail, leading first to Twin Lakes and then to Maxwell Butte, is a trip for the experienced ski tourer, with the crucial factor being snow conditions.

With an adequate snow pack plus four to six inches of new snow or powder, the run out from Twin Lakes becomes a challenging experience. The trail is winding in nature and relatively steep, and double-poling plus occasional step-turns are all that are necessary for the majority of the trip under good conditions. As the ski season progresses, tree-wells become more pronounced and the difficulty of the tour increases. Defensive activities in the form of good route finding on the way up should be taken to avoid unscheduled stops on the way out.

The tour begins on Forest Service Road 1379 on the east side of Oregon 22 about 2¾ miles north of the junction of Oregon 22 and U.S. 20. The junction is known locally as the Santiam "Y."

Parking for two or three vehicles is normally plowed at the intersection of Oregon 22 and FS1379. Follow FS 1379 east for one-half mile to reach the trailhead. It ends in a logged unit. The trail begins on the eastern edge of the clearcut where it enters heavy timber. A Forest Service trail sign marking the trail's starting point is usually visible.

From the timber's edge the first mile of trail is a former jeep road; hence, it is wider and more open than conventional trail. At the 1½ mile mark the trail begins in earnest and progresses gradually until it reaches Twin Lakes. The trail to Twin Lakes is in the trees for its entire length, but upon reaching the lakes it breaks out into open meadows with nearby ridges offering nice runs for those who care to climb them. Mt. Jefferson is visible to the northeast.

Most day tours halt at the lakes; however, forays toward Maxwell Butte, Berley Lakes and Jack Shelter are also possible.

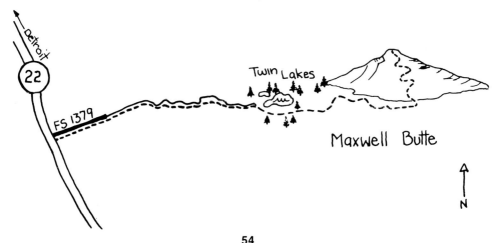

iron mountain

Trail tour
3 miles round-trip
Willamette National Forest
Sweet Home Ranger District
Map: Echo Mountain Quadrangle

Iron Mountain is a tough tour. There are no two ways about it. It is abrupt and tricky.

For a short tour (total length is only 1½ miles) it is extremely deceiving. Perhaps the elevation gain is the best clue to its abruptness. It is tricky because there are a few minor problems such as: 1) finding the trail, 2) following the trail, and 3) getting down.

To attack problem "1," drive east from Eugene 75 miles to the junction of U.S. Highways 20 and 126. At this junction turn west as if going to Sweet Home on U.S. 20, and proceed 9 miles, stopping three-quarters of a mile beyond Tombstone Prairie at Tombstone Summit. A turnout on the south side of the pass provides space for four vehicles. Iron Mountain is slightly northwest of this point.

To find the trail, walk 100 yards west of the parking area, downhill toward Sweet Home. Cross the highway to the north and ski parallel to the highway while looking for a telephone line that runs up the hill to the lookout station that occupies Iron Mountain's summit. The trail in its lower stretches runs beneath the telephone line, but on the upper slopes of the mountain the route becomes obvious and it is unnecessary to follow the line.

The trail for the first mile winds through big timber and several enormous, house-sized boulders (pieces of Iron Mountain which have crumbled away in bygone centuries). At the mile mark, the route breaks out into an open bowl-shaped meadow. From the entry point at the lower end, the trail traverses the meadow diagonally from south to north-west. The traverse ends in a saddle with an open area (a clearcut in summer) visible to the west and north and with Iron Mountain looming to the northeast. A road comes up from the canyon below and ends at a garage in the middle of the clearcut. The roof of the garage is usually exposed, unless the snow is too deep. Also visible from the saddle area is the small cubicle of the lookout station high atop Iron Mountain.

Three options are available: 1) either leave your skis at the saddle and hike up; 2) ski part way up, then leave your skis; or 3) ski all the way up. If you elect to ski all the way you should possess some downhill techniques, or be well-practiced at such things as kick-turns and traverses.

In summer the trail switch-backs up the now obvious open slope on the south-west side of the mountain and only goes to the north side a short distance below the summit. A degree of experience at this point is advisable and the tourer should take care to evaluate snow conditions in terms of both iciness and the possibility of avalanche. The route should switchback through the trees as much as possible. You should exercise caution because of the steep drop-offs in several places, particularly if your traverses are extended too far south.

Finally, just below the summit the trail swings around to the north of the mountain and the skier must take extreme care because huge cornices develop and icy conditions occur. If the skis are left at this point (advisable), poles should be taken for the trip to the top.

Views from the top extend from Mt. Hood in the north to Diamond Peak in the south. On clear days, Mary s Peak in the coast range west of Corvallis can be seen.

Iron Mountain

20

Tomb-
stone
summit

57

potato hill

Road tour
4 miles round-trip
Willamette National Forest
McKenzie Ranger District
Map: Three Fingered Jack Quadrangle

Potato Hill offers the new skier a gently rising road tour and, while altitude is gained, the grade is moderate.

Psychologically, the tour is sound. Two miles of uphill slogging in the morning are rewarded with 2 miles of downhill sliding on the return. On clear days views of the surrounding peaks highlight the uphill march. Logged-over areas ("Units" to use the Forest Service designation) provide unmarred bowls for play and practice.

To reach Potato Hill, drive east from the Willamette Valley to Santiam "Y," the junction of Oregon 22 and U.S. 20, 5½ miles west of Santiam Pass. From the junction proceed east 0.9 of a mile on U.S. 20 to the sharp curve just preceeding the long straightaway down to Lost Lake.

The route up Potato Hill, Jack Pine Road 1371A, begins on the south side of this corner. Parking on the shoulder is usually available for two to four vehicles except during heavy snowstorms, when the shoulder is not plowed and the nearest parking is one-half mile farther east adjacent to Lost Lake. Simply ski back on the north shoulder and cross the highway.

Jack Pine Road, broad and without obstacles, proceeds south for one-quarter mile; then, east and up for 1¾ miles. Offering long, open runs on the return, the road passes through two clearcuts and ends in a third unit. Round trip is approximately 4 miles.

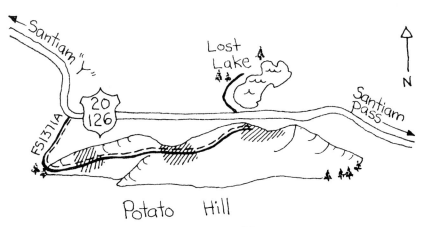

Potato Hill

59

lost lake

Road tour
2 miles round-trip
Willamette National Forest
Detroit Ranger District
Map: Mt. Jefferson Wilderness Area (free from U.S. Forest Service)

The Lost Lake ski tour, located on U.S. 126-20 on the way to Santiam Pass, is an excellent choice for anyone first attempting touring. Because of the lake's exposed position, winds pack snow quickly, which makes an excellent flat surface for practice sessions close to the highway. As with all lakes, however, the skier should take care to ensure that the ice is actually solid, particularly early and late during the year and during the warming periods.

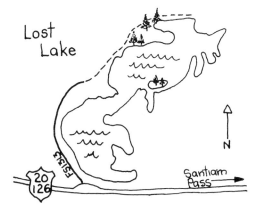

A trip along the lakeshore and through the trees will bring you to a short road which provides summer access to campsites on the north lakeside.

When you go to Lost Lake, the best advice is simply to enjoy yourself. Touring possibilities lend themselves to the desires of the individuals involved. Easy skiing over gently rolling terrain around the lakeshore is the mainstay for beginners, while more experienced people may enjoy forays through the trees.

To get to Lost Lake, head towards Santiam Pass via U.S. 20 or 126 or Oregon 22. At the Santiam "Y," junction of highways 126, 20 and 22, continue east towards the summit for 1½ miles. Lost Lake parallels the highway on the north side, and ample parking is available along the northern roadside.

jack shelter

Trail tour
4½ miles round-trip
Willamette National Forest
Detroit Ranger District
Map: Mt. Jefferson Wilderness Area
(free from U.S. Forest Service)

The trail to Jack Shelter provides trail skiing in the best sense of the sport. It is very definitely a cross-country course. Rolling terrain, which offers good runs both going in and coming out, is predominant throughout the route. Aside from a rather steep one-half mile at the very beginning, the trail offers few problems for the intermediate tourer. The only technical problem to be encountered is finding Jack Shelter.

Leave cars in the parking lot at Santiam Lodge across from the Hoodoo Ski Bowl on the north side of U.S. 20. The trail begins at the north edge of the lot and proceeds up the hill 100 yards northeast. It tops out at the half-mile mark, passes a distinct open area in the trees, a small marsh or tarn in the summer, and proceeds along its eastern boundary in a northerly direction. From this point the trail climbs gradually with ups and downs and crosses several water-courses which should be negotiated with care.

At the 1¾ mile point the trail, previously easy to follow via tree blazes, breaks into more open country and swings northwest. It is advisable to consult contour maps as a passage must be made between several tree-free hillocks, after which the trail resumes heading northwest through the forest. Previous parties have flagged trees with marking tape, and, if visible, these guideposts may set you in the right direction, though many flagged trails in the area go places other than Jack Shelter.

Once you gain the trees on the far side of the meadows, a brief one-half mile ski brings you to Jack Shelter. The shelter is in adequate shape; however, thoughtless users have destroyed many of the existing plank bunks. Adequate firewood can be found nearby. During heavy winters, digging may be required to enter the shelter and a light snow shovel of the backpacking variety is essential.

Author's Note: During April of 1972 the "thoughtless users" previously mentioned finished their work at Jack Shelter and left an unattended campfire which eventually damaged interior and primary timbers to the extent that repair is impossible. Under current statutes governing management of U.S. Forest Service Wilderness Areas, no new shelters can be constructed.

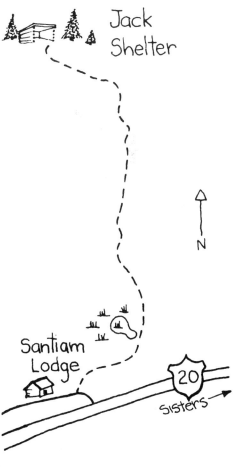

pacific crest trail

Trail tour
3-7 miles round trip
Willamette National Forest
Detroit Ranger District
Map: Three Fingered Jack Quadrangle
- Mt. Jefferson Wilderness Area
   (free from the Forest Service)

The Pacific Crest Trail (formerly called the Skyline Trail), famed route for summer backpackers, offers an equally spectacular journey for winter travelers. In addition to its easy accessibility, its elevation is such that snow comes early and stays late in relation to other touring sites, and when somewhat sloppy conditions plague lower elevations, good snow can often be found by heading up the Crest.

The trail, visible early in the season, becomes increasingly hard to find as the snows progress, and in the spring the best advice is simply to ski north, ski uphill and consult maps. The trailhead is on the north side of U.S. 126-20 at Santiam Pass, three-quarters of a mile east of the Hoodoo Ski Bowl turnoff. Parking is available along the broad south shoulder of the highway itself. Cross the highway and ski north on a short, snowed-in access roadway to the trailhead.

Directly north of the pass, about 1½ miles from the highway and beginning about 5300′ elevation, there are large open meadows. For orientation purposes the Skyline Trail lies west of these meadows.

From the meadows, views south and west are spectacular, and Mt. Washington and the Hoodoo-Hayrick complex loom nearby. While many tours often terminate upon reaching the meadows, longer tours are possible by continuing north along the divide toward Three Fingered Jack. Because of the somewhat substantial gain in elevation (1,000′ in 2 miles), some downhill touring skills are in order.

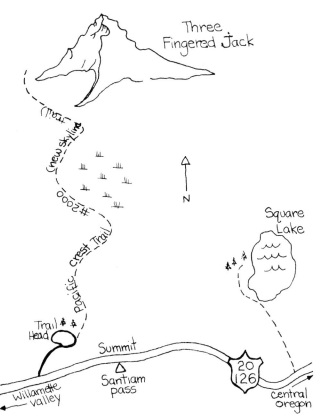

Three Fingered Jack

(new skyline Trail)

Pacific - Crest Trail #2000

N

Square Lake

Trail Head

Summit

Santiam pass

20 126

Willamette valley

central oregon

square lake

Trail tour
3 miles round-trip
Deschutes National Forest
Sisters Ranger District
Map: Mt. Jefferson Wilderness Area
  (free from U.S. Forest Service)

Lying slightly east of Santiam Pass and offering an imposing view of Three Fingered Jack on a clear day, Square Lake is an enjoyable tour for any one from beginner to expert.

The lake is on the north side of a low but steep ridge paralleling U.S. 20, east of Hoodoo Ski Bowl on Santiam Summit. The tour, which is only 1 mile to the lake, is a short one. Terrain, however, is varied, and after climbing steeply for one-half mile to reach the ridge top, you will suddenly find yourself descending the steep slope to the lake on the opposite side.

The trail is heavily forested but lacks major underbrush. This tour is possible for the beginner as well as the more advanced skier since it is possible to negotiate the steep north side through a series of long, gentle traverses. The skier with more downhill experience usually takes a more direct route.

Skiing on the lake, provided it is safely frozen, is excellent, and good views of Three Fingered Jack are possible once you leave the trees. In addition, for those ski tourers with downhill instincts, several open slopes on the north and west sides of the lake offer nice runs.

To arrive at the trailhead, drive 2½ miles east of the turn-off to Hoodoo Ski Bowl on U.S. 20 on Santiam Pass, and watch for a sign reading "Summit Trail" on the south side of the highway pointing north. The route to Square Lake goes north. Often, no parking space will be available at the trailhead. The nearest parking generally available is at a turnout on the south side of the highway one-half mile farther east.

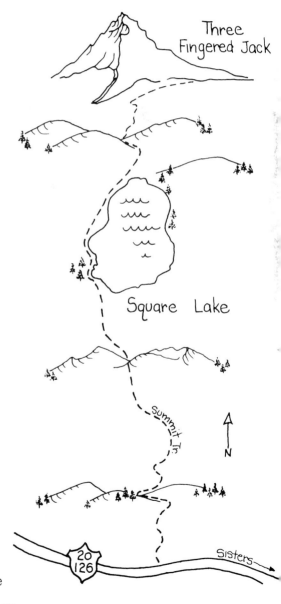

blue lake trail

Trail tour
3 miles (one-way downhill)
Deschutes National Forest
Sisters Ranger District
Map: Three Fingered Jack Quadrangle

For that certain breed of ski tourer who is, in reality, a frustrated downhiller, the Blue Lake Trail is a fine compromise of both worlds. Located 3 miles east of the Hoodoo Ski Bowl turn-off on San-

tiam Summit, the trail is virtually all downhill with a few somewhat level spots for the contemplation of nature or the changing of waxes. Tour length is 3 miles.

The starting point is a prominent turn-out one-half mile east of the "Summit Trail" sign on U.S. 126-20. This turn-out is plowed, and space is available to park five cars. The trail is located on the south side of the highway about fifty yards down the hill below the turn-out. With a large amount of snow it may be difficult to find; however, even with snow a definite defile is visible and trees sport trimmed branches and blaze marks.

The trail (in actuality a jeep road) runs gradually downhill for its entire length and passes through several open areas which offer a number of fairly long, semi-open runs through the trees. After 2 miles the jeep road/trail abruptly ends, and you emerge in a maze of logging roads, many of which are not marked. At this point it is up to you to evaluate your situation and pick an appropriate route downhill, while realizing that the trail parallels the highway and that the idea is to eventually funnel down between the highway and Blue Lake.

Toward the end of the 3 miles and shortly before reaching Blue Lake, the terrain flattens out and a plateau of sorts parallels a deep gorge containing a stream which eventually flows into the lake. The plateau ends as it meets the ridge sloping down from the north to Blue Lake. In the interest of safety you should carry adequate maps of the area showing new logging roads and points of access and exit.

Procedure now calls for the only climbing of the day, a somewhat arduous one-half-mile back up the hill to regain U.S. 126-20. From there, it is a short hitchhike for drivers back to the vehicles, or by planning ahead, one vehicle can be left at a turnout within sight of Blue Lake (it is visible from the highway on any but an extremely foul day), and drivers can be transferred for the shuttle.

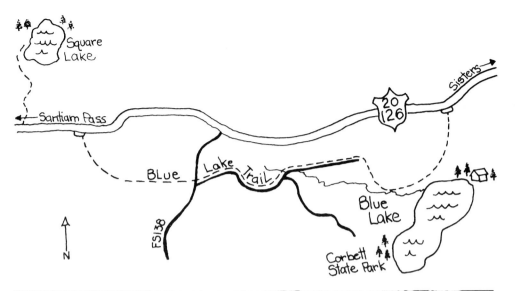

hoodoo meadows

Road tour
2 miles round-trip
Willamette National Forest
McKenzie Ranger District
Map: Three Fingered Jack Quadrangle

Heard about ski touring? Like to try it, but don't want to take on anything overly complicated the first time out?

Try Hoodoo Meadows.

No, the above is not a come-on for some fast-buck, ski tour promoter. It could be. Hoodoo Meadows has so many positive things going for it in terms of catering to those trying touring for the first time that there is nothing to do but list them:

1.) You start at Hoodoo Ski Bowl which is not hard to find.
2.) Total round-trip distance is only two miles.
3.) Rental equipment is available at the ski area.
4.) It is a road tour, gently rolling, plus meadows.
5.) You are a quarter-mile from a plowed roadway at all times, though you won't know it because of the dense timber, unless you seek it out.
6.) You can make the tour and return to the lodge in time for lunch.

Admittedly, the conveniences associated with this tour are exceptional. For downhill skiers who want to try touring for an afternoon, or those people who want a trip which offers fewer formalities than the majority of tours, Hoodoo Meadows is ideal.

To begin the tour, go to the main lodge at Hoodoo Ski Bowl, which is located at Santiam Pass on U.S. 126-20. The trail begins in the trees on the northern edge of the ski area. To find it, look north from the lodge to the wedge-shaped "bunny hill" area between the ski area's two rope tows. Midway between the uphill terminals of the two tows there is an orange snow-depth marking post at the edge of the timber. The trail, an access and fire road in summer, begins near this marker. It continues north from the area, passes a pumphouse and eventually travels through several large meadows and ends in the largest meadow a dozen feet from U.S. 20. The highway is not visible because of a fringe of trees. The trail is marked occasionally by metal orange tags nailed to trees, and it parallels the access road to the ski area, which lies a quarter mile to the east.

The meadows, broad and flat, offer good opportunities to improve technique through practice on easily constructed circular tracks. To return to the ski area, merely retrace your steps.

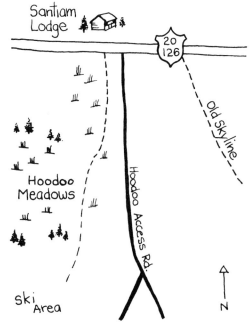

hoodoo-big lake

Road tour
4-6 miles average
Willamette National Forest
McKenzie Ranger District
Map: Three Fingered Jack Quadrangle

It is with some reservation that we discuss ski touring in the vicinity of Hoodoo and Big Lake. The problem in advising anyone of the desirability of going into this area for touring purposes comes down to matters of personal philosophy and purism.

Hoodoo and Big Lake, at one time a ski tourer's paradise, have declined rapidly in pleasure within recent years. The primary reason for this is the tremendous boom in the popularity of snowmobiling. The Big Lake region, from Cache Mountain on the east to Sand Mountain on the west, and most notably on the road from the Hoodoo parking lot to Big Lake (a distance of 2 miles), is a veritable hotbed of snowmobile activity. What was at one time a great tour, one of the best for first-time ski tourers, has now turned into a drag strip for easy-chair sportsmen, and tours through this area have lost much of their appeal.

Perhaps, if Big Lake and surrounding environs are still desirable, the best route into the country in view of the snowmobile problems lies between Hayrick and Hoodoo Buttes. The ski to the saddle between the two buttes starts at the bottom of the red chair lift, up the small bunny hill, and, when visible, follows the road which extends up between the two mountains. From the saddle the route goes through a section of burned-over forest from the Big Lake Airstrip fire of 1967. Because of some steepness of terrain, traverses may be in order, though some long runs through the trees are available.

Once upon the flats, you may travel through the basically open burn area toward Big Lake and return to Hoodoo via the Big Lake Road (in effect, circling Hayrick Butte), or retrace the route back to the saddle.

On occasion touring can also take place within the bounds of Hoodoo Ski Bowl. On an off-day (usually during the week, not weekends) when new snow, hopefully powder, blankets the area, the early arriver is treated to some incredibly-fun downhill runs through virgin white-stuff, before sno-cats manage to manicure the tourer out of existence. A good route to the upper reaches, near and above the blue chair, extends up the northern edge of the area and follows the edge around via broad runs which end at the blue chair. From the blue chair, a road runs south to southwest along the ridgeline, and, if followed in its entirety, ends at the green chair terminal on the top of Hoodoo Butte.

Hoodoo Ski Bowl and Big Lake Basin are located at Santiam Pass on U.S 126-20 about 85 miles east of Eugene, and about 75 miles southeast of Salem.

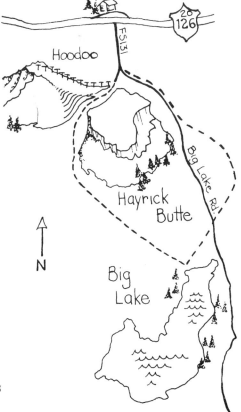

sand mountain traverse

Road and trail tour
8-9 miles (one-way)
Willamette National Forest
McKenzie Ranger District
Map: Three Fingered Jack and Echo Mountain Quadrangles

The Sand Mountain Traverse, beginning at Hoodoo Ski Bowl and ending at Fish Lake on the Clear Lake cut-off, is a tour designed for good conditions and skiers with a fair amount of experience. It is, for the most part, almost all flat land or downhill touring and, depending on route variations, is 8 to 9 miles in length.

Starting point for the tour is the red chair at Hoodoo Ski Bowl on Santiam Pass 85 miles east of Eugene. From the base of the red chair, ski south, uphill, and travel through the natural pass between Hoodoo and Hayrick Buttes. Once the saddle is made, the drop down to the flats adjacent to Big Lake becomes evident and the route, maintaining elevation and not descending into the trees, traverses the back side of Hoodoo Butte.

As you contour around the Butte, you will find the flats west of Big Lake become visible. They end at Sand Mountain, a two-humped cinder cone at the western edge of the 1967 Big Lake burn, on which sits Sand Mountain Lookout, a small structure usually visible on the southern-most summit. Objective at this point is the north side of Sand Mountain and a natural pass which exists between Sand Mountain and some cinder cones to the north. From the south slope of Hoodoo Butte, a natural line-of-sight course to the pass area is easily plotted. By staying to the northern edge of the flats, you can ski a route that is level or downhill.

As you traverse the flats, you will encounter a roadway, the old Santiam Wagon Road. Once found, it can be followed to the Clear Lake cut-off. If the Wagon Road is not easily discernable, proceed to the pass area where it is fairly obvious. The road to the summit of Sand Mountain heads up and westward around the northern cone. (Side trip: it is approximately 1 mile to the summit of Sand Mountain plus an elevation gain of 775 feet from the Wagon Road junction.)

From the junction proceed west, climb briefly on a small hill, and then begin the final drop which extends all the way through to the Clear Lake cut-off. The runs are often long and open and the road/trail is fairly obvious. If you lose it, backtrack to the last point that you were on it; then, check trees for telephone wire insulators, which are evident for most of the route.

One and one-half miles past Sand Mountain an intersection with Forest Service Road 1370 is evident and a choice in route becomes necessary. You can either continue on the Santiam Wagon Road or follow FS1370, a broad thoroughfare. Both routes lead to Clear Lake cut-off three-quarters to 1 mile south of Fish Lake. Fish Lake is a necessary orientation point because the turnout to Fish Lake Work Center is the only area in the vicinity plowed by snowplows which allows a vehicle to get off the road. One vehicle can be left at this site and drivers can be shuttled back to the parking lot at Hoodoo. Time for the tour under average conditions is five to six hours.

fish lake

Road tour
3 miles round-trip
Willamette National Forest
McKenzie Ranger District
Map: Echo Mountain Quadrangle

For a longer tour, follow the lake-bed west to a marshy area where Hackleman Creek drains into Fish Lake. From this point you will see a clearcut, slightly southwest, running from the lakeshore up the ridge and perpendicular to the lake. Three Fingered Jack and the crest of the Cascades are visible from the top.

Fish Lake, a site of former importance to early-day trans-Cascades travelers, offers a tour with historic as well as scenic possibilities, ideally suited to the first-time tourer.

The setting, west of Santiam Pass on the Clear Lake cut-off, was a major interchange for persons journeying east or west through the mountains along the old Santiam Wagon Road. A number of buildings, some still remaining, occupied the site. Around the turn of the century the U.S. Forest Service established a remount station there to handle the livestock needs of its men and packstrings. During the summer months, the Fish Lake Work Center still functions in this capacity.

To reach Fish Lake, drive to the junction of U.S. 20 and U.S. 126, six miles west of Santiam Pass. Fish Lake lies on the west side of the highway 1 mile south of that junction. In winter, access to the area is via the only plowed turnout anywhere in the vicinity, where the road into Fish Lake Work Center, FS 1364, intersects the cut-off.

Depending upon how much has been plowed, space is usually available for two to three cars, and efforts should be made to consolidate riders before leaving the city.

From the starting point the tour down into the Work Center is a short one-quarter mile. Old log cabins dot the hillside and Fish Lake is a short distance away. When sufficient snow and ice cover the lake, skiing on its broad surface is possible and all manner of touring techniques can be practiced.

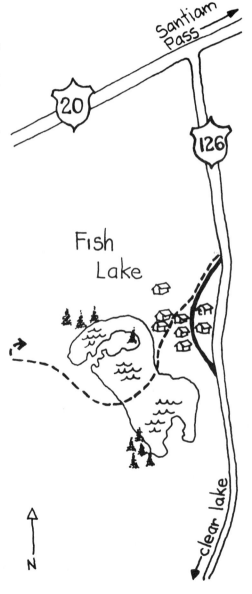

smith prairie

Road tour
2¾ miles round-trip
Willamette National Forest
McKenzie Ranger District
Map: Echo Mountain Quadrangle

Smith Prairie is simply a name for a basic place you might wind up. It sounds better than "Forest Service Road 1465." Touring on FS1465 may take you to Smith Prairie; then again, it might not. At any rate, it is a good tour for anyone spending time in the Clear Lake area.

FS1465 is a logging road. The grade is gentle, and along its route you encounter numerous clearcuts, which under seven feet of snow look much the same as Smith Prairie itself. Depending upon snow conditions, some nice runs may be made in these units. Several creeks, including Ikenick Creek, offer photographic possibilities as their waters wind through snow-banked channels.

Smith Prairie is there, somewhere north of the junction of roads FS1465 and

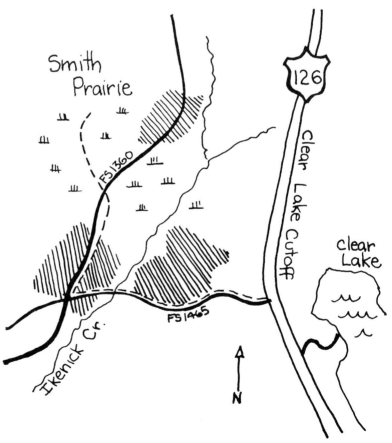

FS1360. Precisely where is unimportant. Getting to Smith Prairie is not really the reason this trip is recommended. Rather, it is an escape from the maddening crowd. It is a tour away from the crest, away from the higher reaches which often are crowded. It is a roadhead, a place to start. Once you arrive at that point, where you go is purely up to you.

Jumping off point for Smith Prairie and beyond is located at the junction of Road 1465 and U.S. 126, a hundred yards or so north of the main entrance to Clear Lake. To get there, drive east of Eugene on U.S. 126 or east of Sweet Home on U.S. 20. Clear Lake lies 4 miles south of the junction of 126-20. It is well marked.

clear lake

Road tour
1 mile round-trip
Willamette National Forest
McKenzie Ranger District
Map: Three Fingered Jack Quadrangle

Clear Lake, a prominent and well-known destination for many summer visitors to the Oregon Cascades, is also a suitable objective for people seeking a worthwhile winter outing. Consider the following objectives:

Trip length is short. From the car to the lake's edge it is no more than one-half mile.

It is virtually all downhill going in.

It is virtually all uphill going out.

There is a large, sturdily-built shelter which offers a fireplace and possible overnight protection for those who want an easy overnight outing.

Finally, touring into a place such as Clear Lake is just something to do as a change of pace. It is a simple tour. It is pleasant for a family with small children looking for a place to picnic on a warm spring day. It is the kind of place to go for an afternoon tour when you wake up at 10 a.m. and still want to go somewhere for a bit of afternoon exercise.

To get to Clear Lake, travel U.S. 126 to the Clear Lake cut-off, that section of U.S. 126 running between the McKenzie and Santiam highways. This is above Clear Lake on a western hillside. The lake lies 4 miles south of the junction of U.S. 20 and 126, 71 miles east of Eugene. It is well-signed and a large turnout accommodating five to seven cars is plowed throughout the winter.

To reach Clear Lake, park at the turnout: ski down the access road into the campground. Because of the lake's low elevation (3012'), there are hazards from thin ice or over-hung cornices and the skier should be cautious.

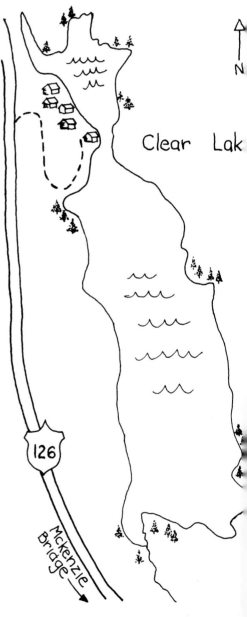

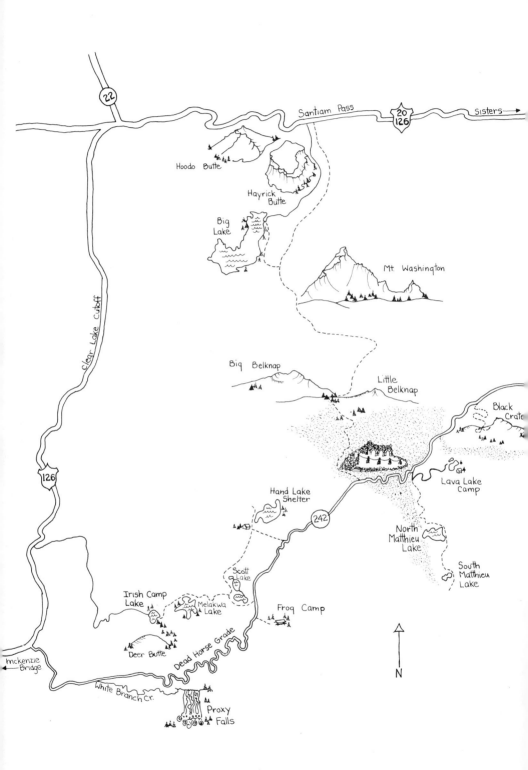

mckenzie pass tours

McKenzie Pass is an historic east-west route which at one time was the major link between eastern and western communities in the central part of the state. In the early days, when snow blocked the pass each winter, travel east to west was virtually at a standstill until the spring thaw. Skiing played a vital role in the 1870's when an early-day mailman, John Templeton Craig, attempted to carry the mail across McKenzie Pass in the dead of winter using skis. In recent years all-weather routes have been forged over the Willamette and Santiam Passes and the McKenzie Highway, now designated a scenic route, is usually forgotten by most people from December to July when closed by snow.

The fact that McKenzie Pass is shut down—blocked off with large orange gates—is the unique factor which makes touring in the area a little out of the ordinary. For many seasoned tourers in the central part of the state, the pass is the place to both start and end the touring season. For those people who simply CAN'T WAIT, even for Thanksgiving which is the traditional opening date for the general ski season, ski touring can commence as early as mid-October. But you must be willing to carry your skis several miles to the open meadows which receive the first snow on the upper slopes of Black Crater at the 6,000 foot level.

Similarly, in mid-June it is possible to leave your car near McKenzie Pass and hike south into the Three Sisters Wilderness Area for some pleasurable runs in the good corn snow on the slopes of the Middle Sister.

Once the first snows begin, in the fall, the McKenzie Highway usually remains open for a period of about a week, or until plowing becomes an unreasonable chore for the Highway Department.

This is the signal for a few brief flings before the gates close. Matthieu Lakes trail is good. Millican Crater trail can be fun, or a brief run into Hand Lake Shelter is invigorating. But don't put it off. At the first hint of snow, go. If you wait too long the gates shut which means long approach marches or a forced wait until July.

The long approach march is the other side of touring on McKenzie Pass. Ski touring across the pass on the highway has been popular for a considerable time. It began in the 1920's or 30's and was eventually commemorated into a ski race honoring John Craig. This event has been instituted several times and was recently rejuvenated in 1970 with the new interest in ski touring. It is now sponsored by the Oregon Nordic Club and held annually, usually in April. Both cross-country racers and ski tourers participate.

A multitude of long-distance, multi-day tours are possible in the area. Several parties have traversed the Three Sisters, beginning at Mt. Bachelor and ending at Whitebranch. Another long tour is from Hoodoo Ski Bowl south across the Mt. Washington Wilderness Area to McKenzie Highway. Many other lengthy tours are possible for individuals who are skilled, equipped and can spare a few days.

McKenzie Pass is perhaps best suited for those individuals who are more than just casually interested in ski touring. It is ideal for those who want to begin early and ski late. When the pass closes, the sheer size and distance involved thins out the pack and separates the casual day tourer from individuals interested in testing themselves against a challenging and sometimes hostile environment.

irish camp lake

Road tour
6-18 miles round-trip
Willamette National Forest
McKenzie Ranger District
Map: Three Sisters Quadrangle and
McKenzie Ranger District U.S. F.S.

Irish Camp Lake is a novelty tour. It is an example of what is available if you take the trouble to forge off the beaten path and investigate likely looking places. It is representative, then, of the great number of hidden, undiscovered tours, there for your exploration.

The unique factor about Irish Camp Lake and the lands adjacent to it is winter access. Because of a large amount of timber harvesting in the Scott Creek drainage, back roads are plowed during early winter snow storms. The snow eventually wins out, but during the early months of the season, touring country is available that is later many miles from plowed highways.

Irish Camp Lake lies northeast of Deer Butte and west of Melakwa Lake. Primary route in is by Forest Service Road 1601. To get to FS1601, travel to the junction of U.S. 126 and Oregon 242, 4½ miles east of McKenzie Bridge. Proceed 3 miles northeast on U.S. 126 to the first intersecting road on the right side of the highway beyond the Belknap Springs junction. This is FS 1601.

Drive up FS1601 as far as possible or start skiing at the highway. Irish Camp Lake is 9 miles east by road from the junction.

The tour is simple, the only limiting factor being the length. It is primarily a road tour but a number of clearcuts offer interesting variations. A possible approach deviation exists for parties skiing east-to-west across McKenzie Pass. By taking a detour at Scott Lake and following the road to Melakwa Lake, a trail ski of one-half mile brings tourers to Irish Camp Lake and a snowed-in road system. You could then avoid heavy weekend snowmobile use on the lower reaches of Oregon 242 near Whitebranch Youth Camp.

85

proxy falls

Road and trail tour
6 miles round-trip
Willamette National Forest
McKenzie Ranger District
Map: Three Sisters Wilderness
(free from the Forest Service)

Proxy Falls, a series of high waterfalls on the northern edge of the Three Sisters Wilderness Area, is an ideal goal for ski tourers on a single-day outing. Tour length is 6 miles round-trip.

Except for the last one-half mile the tour to the falls is basically a road tour. The route follows the Old McKenzie Highway (Oregon 242) for 2½ miles, then continues on a trail the remaining one-half mile to two view points overlooking the falls.

Under most conditions, you can ski within close range of the falls, though during some periods ice may build up and skis should be left at a lower level below the viewpoints.

To get to the trailhead, drive to Mc-Kenzie Bridge, 50 miles east of Eugene on U.S. 126. 4½ miles east of McKenzie Bridge you reach a junction with Oregon 242. U.S. 126 continues north up the Clear Lake cut-off. Follow Oregon 242 east toward McKenzie Pass. The road is plowed 7½ miles farther to Whitebranch Youth Camp where the tour begins. Ski up the snowed-in highway. The final one-half mile of trail to the falls departs from the south side of the highway and is well marked.

Proxy Falls is a good tour for weekdays. On weekends during mid-winter, snowmobiles can be a problem and other tours may be more rewarding. From the parking area at Whitebranch, distance to the falls is 3 miles one-way. With the spring sun, the distance shortens.

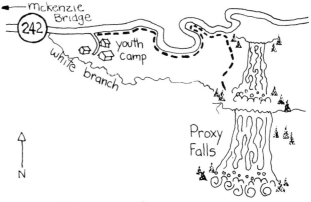

hand lake shelter

Road tour with some trail skiing
12-14 miles round-trip
Willamette National Forest
McKenzie Ranger District
Map: Three Sisters Quadrangle

The trip to Hand Lake Shelter, whether a day tour or an over-night, is best done in mid-spring when sufficient warm periods have melted snow at lower elevations and the Old McKenzie Highway (Oregon 242) is open to the snow gate at Alder Springs Campground.

Length of this tour, depending on routes taken, is between 12 and 14 miles round-trip. Basic procedure is to ski up Oregon 242 beyond the snow gate. This section of the road, known locally as Deadhorse Grade (at times bare of snow in several places during warm periods), lasts for 3 miles until you reach the long flats near Frog Camp and Scott Lake.

At the Scott Lake turn-off, several options are available. You may either:

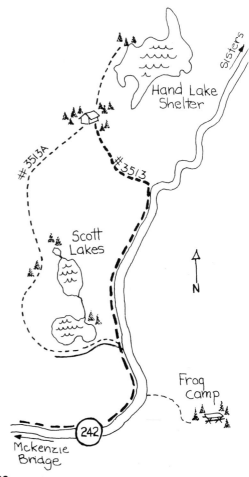

1.) Ski up the highway another 1¼ miles and take a short trail on the west side of the highway one-half mile into Hand Lake; 2.) Ski to Scott Lake or across it, and then pick up the blazes along trail FS3513A on the west and north sides of the lake. This trail proceeds northeast to Hand Lake, first among the trees and then entering open flats; 3.) Follow the first choice, but instead of returning the same way, continue south from Hand Lake Shelter to Scott Lake and loop back to 242.

No matter which option you select a major problem may be in finding the shelter. It is located in a stand of trees on a finger of the south side of the lake. To get there via option one, follow the one-half mile trail from the highway down a small stream course which runs into Hand Lake. Stay on the south edge of this stream until it runs into large flats.

Under eight feet of snow it is often hard to tell when you are actually on the lake or on the shore, but when you finally reach the lake you will be able to look south down a long open flat which runs into trees. Ski down this flat a short distance and you will find the shelter in a cluster of trees on the flat's east side. The other route, FS3513A, follows the flats, enters the timber and eventually reaches Scott Lake.

To reach the snow gate at Alder Springs and the beginning of the tour, drive east of Eugene on U.S. 126 to its junction with Oregon 242. Follow Oregon 242 to the gate or until the road is blocked by snow. A call to the McKenzie Ranger Station during office hours can often provide information concerning snow level and road conditions.

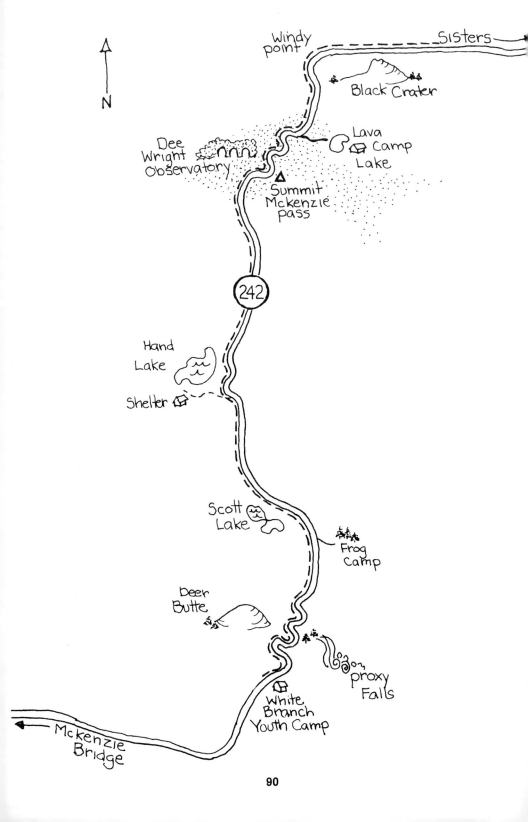

Windy point

Sisters

Black Crater

N

Dee Wright Observatory

Lava Camp Lake

Summit Mckenzie pass

242

Hand Lake

Shelter

Scott Lake

Frog camp

Deer Butte

proxy Falls

White Branch Youth Camp

Mckenzie Bridge

mckenzie pass

Road tour
18-25 miles (one-way)
Willamette and Deschutes National
**   Forests**
McKenzie and Sisters Ranger Districts
Map: Three Sisters Wilderness
**   (free from the Forest Service)**

The ski tour over McKenzie Pass is a trek associated with a touch of stamina and a lot of history. When old-time ski tourers from the 20's and 30's get together (those were the days when touring was skiing—chairlifts weren't invented), talk will often turn to the much-enjoyed tour over McKenzie Pass.

The tour, in fact, was turned into a Nordic Race, the John Craig Memorial Ski Race, honoring John Templeton Craig, an old-time mail carrier who skied mail across the pass in December, 1877. Craig was trapped in a cabin near the summit in a fierce blizzard during his run and died on the spot. A marker commemorating his death is located approximately 2 miles west of the summit.

The race originally occurred in the 1930's, again in the early 50's and has now been rejuvenated by the Oregon Nordic Club who sponsored the race in 1970 as a new annual event open to all comers.

The course of the tour is quite simple. Follow the Old McKenzie Highway, Oregon 242, from west to east or east to west, beginning either at the snow gates or behind them, depending on the snow level. The pass is closed to travel in November or December of each year and is not plowed out until May or June.

Distance between the snow gates is 18 miles.

For the strong skier, the run over the pass is a one-day trip. For skiers unsure of their speed or endurance, however, an easy overnighter can be planned in a comfortable shelter at Lava Camp Lake. To get to the shelter, take the Lava Camp Lake road, three-quarters of a mile east of Dee Wright Observatory on the south side of the highway. The shelter is on the south side of the lake, one-half mile from Oregon 242.

Anyone planning to ski over the pass would to well to watch weather conditions closely and to carry enough gear for an overnight stay, if necessary. Storms can be severe, and large amounts of new snow can be dumped in short periods of time. Generally speaking, the best time to ski the pass is in the spring : March or April.

north matthieu lake

Trail tour
4 miles round-trip
Deschutes National Forest
Sisters Ranger District
Map: Three Sisters Wilderness
(free from the Forest Service)

Tours in the McKenzie Pass region are premium tours. Good scenery, good snow, ideal trails—all combine for desirable outings. For most tourers, however, the available skiing period is short-lived. Such a tour is the trip to North Matthieu Lake. An ideal tour, it is only open for those few short weeks on McKenzie Pass when the snow is deep enough to ski in, but not deep enough for the Highway Department to cease plowing the road.

To get to North Matthieu Lake, drive three-quarters of a mile east of Dee Wright Observatory on McKenzie Pass to the junction of the Lava Camp Lake access road and Oregon 242. Turn off on the access road. The trailhead is 100 yards from the highway on the first right-hand turn-off on the access road. An ample parking lot, featuring a bulletin board and trail sign, is hard to miss.

The trail to North Matthieu, a segment of the Pacific Crest National Scenic Trail (Oregon Skyline Trail), is a broad, easily followed avenue, offering moderate, gentle hills throughout its 2 mile course, with a slightly steeper switchback section prior to reaching the lake.

Because of the early season accessibility of North Matthieu, ice on the lake is not trust-worthy.

For those people with downhill competency, a good hill exists on the east side of the lake, and, if the powder is right, storybook runs are possible. The trail traverses the base of the hill along the shore of the lake and proceeds on to South Matthieu Lake, three-quarters of a mile farther, and a possible destination on an overnight outing.

Views from South Mathieu Lake of the North Sister and surrounding country are spectacular, but the lake, in turn, is in a more exposed position, and North Matthieu is a better location during stormy weather.

black crater

Trail tour
6 miles round-trip
Deschutes National Forest
Sisters Ranger District
Map: Three Sisters Wilderness
         (free from the Forest Service)

Ski touring on Black Crater is an activity for the very young or the very young at heart. It is recommended for those who wish to tour early in the season or to prolong touring until sometime in July.

Black Crater is a 7,251 foot volcanic peak located on the northern edge of the Three Sisters Wilderness area, a dozen miles west of Sisters, Oregon.

A trip up Black Crater, snow or not, is well worth the effort. Though fairly steep—a 2,342 foot elevation gain in 3 miles—the view from the upper reaches is spectacular, with peaks such as Mt. Washington and the Three Sisters looming above the lava flows, and the other major guardians of the crest visible as far as Mt. Adams in Washington.

Black Crater gets early snow. The first flurries can begin near its summit in late September or early October. Skiable snow is usually available on higher slopes (depending on how you define "skiable") by late October, and sizeable patches usually linger on the north and northeast slopes well into the summer.

Access to Black Crater is a problem. When Oregon 242, the route over McKenzie Pass, is open, the trailhead adjoins the highway. It is located east of Dee Wright Observatory, the summit of McKenzie Pass, between mileposts 80 and 81, 50 yards east of a prominent highway curve abutting the lava called Windy Point. The trail begins on the south side of the highway, and parking is available there for several vehicles.

Trail length is 3 miles to the summit. Early in the year, the common practice is to carry skis the first mile or so to meadows near the 5,600 foot level. From that point, the snow gets better as the altitude increases.

Closure of the highway following the first severe storms of the winter, usually in December, halts touring on Black Crater for all but the hardy, those individuals willing to ski in the 4 to 7 miles of approach which are necessary when the snow level drops and the highway is unplowed.

N

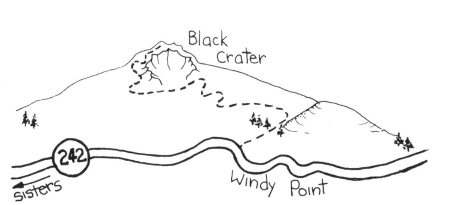

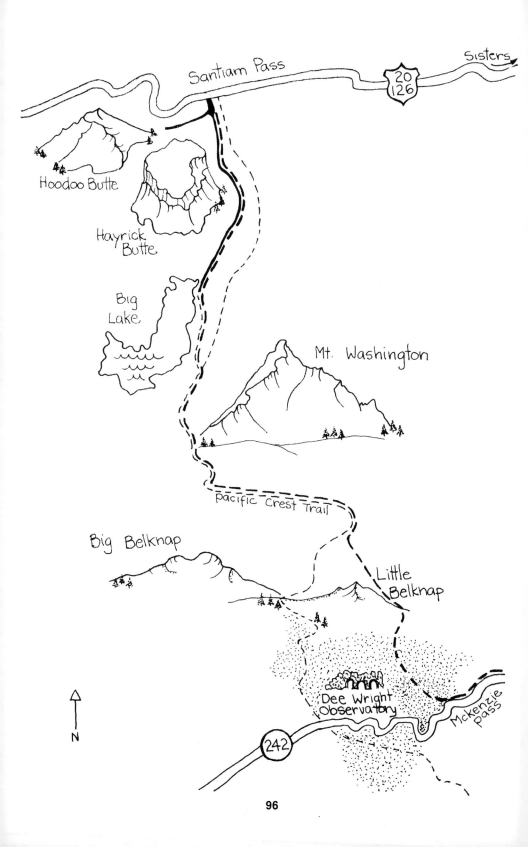

Santiam Pass

Sisters

20
126

Hoodoo Butte

Hayrick Butte

Big Lake

Mt. Washington

Pacific Crest Trail

Big Belknap

Little Belknap

Dee Wright Observatory

McKenzie Pass

242

N

hoodoo to mc kenzie pass

Trail tour
20-22 miles (one-way)
Willamette and Deschutes National Forests
McKenzie and Sisters Ranger Districts
Map: Three Fingered Jack Quadrangle

To ski tour from Hoodoo to the McKenzie Highway in a single day is an ambitious undertaking; a day tour with merit. It is not for the unprepared. Hoodoo to McKenzie Pass is perhaps a tour you will do once, on the way up to bigger, longer and tougher things.

Frankly, it is kind of a grind. The trip is 20 to 22 miles in length, with spring conditions running the spectrum: rock-hard trackless concrete in the morning to pine needle-laced slush in the afternoon, with maybe some volcanic grit and a little tree-drip thrown in along the way for good measure.

But is can also be nice. You start at Hoodoo Ski Bowl at Santiam Pass. From Hoodoo ski south on Forest Service Road 131.1, cross Big Lake and cut up to the Pacific Crest Trail as it passes Mt. Washington. As the trail swings east beyond Washington Ponds, con-tinue due south to the lava. Ski east on the lava until you reach a saddle between Mt. Washington and Belknap Crater. Continue on the east side of Belknap Crater and traverse towards Dee Wright Observatory or merely any section of the McKenzie Highway between Lava Camp Lake and Windy Point. When you reach the highway, ski east and downhill to the snowgate west of Sisters and to a vehicle prudently left there in anticipation of your arrival.

The tour runs through spectacular country. Mt. Washington is nearby for a sizeable portion of the journey and the Three Sisters, as well as other adjacent peaks, come into view as the tour reaches the lava fields.

In contemplating this tour you should consider these factors:

1.) It is a very long tour—20 to 22 miles.

2.) The portion of the tour traversing the west side of Mt. Washington from Big Lake to the lava fields is an endless series of ups and downs. The trail is often hard to find, and numerous ridges running down from the summit make contouring tedious.

3.) Once you reach the lava, the skiing becomes easier; however, in bad weather the lava is a maze, and following the route can be troublesome.

In the final analysis, this tour is a challenge. If you succeed, you know you have accomplished something.

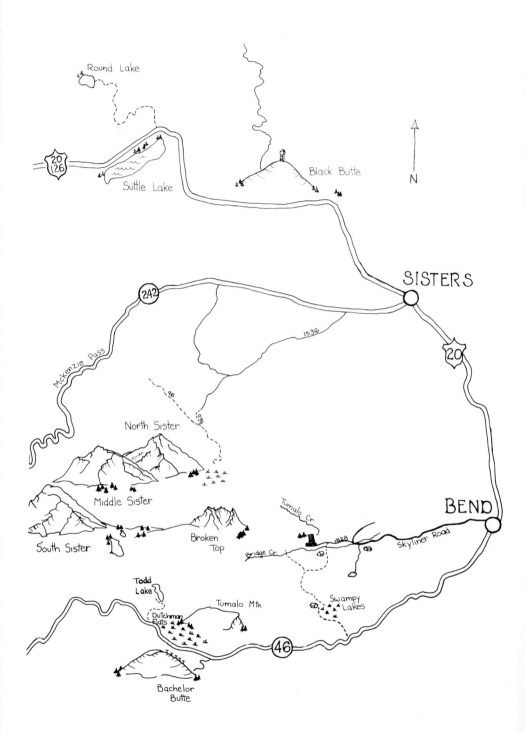

Round Lake

20
126

Suttle Lake

Black Butte

N

SISTERS

242

McKenzie Pass

1536

20

96

North Sister

Middle Sister

South Sister

Broken Top

Tumalo Cr.

1828

Bridge Cr.

Skyliner Road

BEND

Todd Lake

Tumalo Mtn.

Swampy Lakes

Dutchman Flats

46

Bachelor Butte

central oregon tours

The ski tours described in this section are located in the central part of the state on the east side of the Cascades, all within an hour's drive of the Bend city limits. Many are much closer.

For touring enthusiasts on the west side of the Cascades, Bend and its higher, drier, colder climate emanates a definite magnetism. If a west-side tourer can make it to Bend and sample the dry powder two or three times a year, his fortitude is replenished and he can go back and again contend with the wetter, sloppier white stuff more common closer to home.

It is common knowledge that ski tourers residing in Bend have it made. Snow is found within the city on a regular basis and a continual winter-long snow pack is but a few minutes drive west from the business district. A complex of nearby trails offers tours of both short and long duration.

A number of those tours are included in this section. The primary idea is to introduce you to the area. Once you make a few trips, other obvious possibilities should become evident. The Mt. Bachelor/Dutchman Flat vicinity is the jumping-off point for a multitude of tours. Some people merely ski the flats within sight of the lodge. Others go on longer tours to Tumalo Mountain, Todd Lake or Broken Top Crater. And a third typical group goes on much longer trips of many days duration, penetrating the Three Sisters Wilderness and sometimes traversing the mountains to the western side.

One cluster of tours described here is located north of Bend, west of the town of Sisters. From all reports very few people are ski touring in this area. Three to five feet of snow often exists on the eastern foothills of the Cacades and the cold temperatures coupled with the occasional tendency toward clearing and periods of good weather make this a site worthy of further investigation.

A number of other trips contained in other sections of this book, such as those near the summits of Santiam, McKenzie and Willamette Passes are as accessible to Central Oregon residents as they are to their west-side counterparts. Boundary lines established arbitrarily for purposes of organization and groupings should not be taken too seriously, since many areas overlap.

black butte - metolius river

Road and trail tours
2 mi./10 mi./14 mi. round-trips,
**   depending on tour**
Deschutes National Forest
Sisters Ranger District
Maps: Sisters and Three Fingered
**   Jack Quadrangles**

Ski touring in the Black Butte—Metolius River region, a moderately arid, central Oregon setting of small pine thickets among towering Ponderosas, offers numerous touring opportunities ranging from easy trips of several hours to a winter ascent of Black Butte.

The primary area lies west of the town of Sisters, surrounding the resort community of Camp Sherman. Camp Sherman is accessible year around via a paved road extending north from U.S. 20. The Metolius River, a famous fly-fishing stream, flows from the base of Black Butte, a 6,436 foot cinder cone which dominates the area and offers views from its summit of the entire crest of the Cascades from the Three Sisters to Mt. Adams in Washington.

In the area around Camp Sherman, numerous Forest Service fire roads offer ample touring possibilities, and a powerline right-of-way, extending southwest from Camp Sherman to Suttle Lake, is also inviting. Following are three typical tours representative of the area:

Powerline Loop —
This short tour, no more than 2 miles, offers some conditioning exercise for long trips or a brief tour before dinner. To arrive at the starting point, drive to the junction of former Forest Service Road 1317 and U.S. 20, located at the eastern end of Suttle Lake and recently closed to motorized travel. It is directly across U.S. 20 from the Suttle Lake Picnic Area, a day-use campground. Parking space is usually plowed on both sides of the highway. Because there is a blind corner just west of the junction, you should exercise extreme caution when crossing the highway.

Follow FS1317 north for 50 yards, until a powerline is visible coming across the road from the right or east. Veer off the road and follow the powerline downhill for 1 mile. The terrain is gently rolling with several pleasant

runs. The line will eventually cross FS 1210, at which point you should turn left or north.

FS1210 may be plowed, and if so, parallel the road heading north for 100 yards to FS1317. Follow FS1317 uphill and southwest to regain the starting point. The only possible point of confusion lies at the Round Lake Road junction where FS1319 meets FS1317. To return to U.S. 20, take the left or southwest fork. At major road junctions the route is well marked.

Black Butte—
Ski touring possibilities on Black Butte are many. While hearty souls with down-hill skiing experience and/or courage may desire to try for the top, other individuals with less monumental ambitions can enjoy themselves on the lower road which circles the butte, or cut their own trails through the open glades and gentle, sloping terrain which is characteristic of the butte's lower northern slopes.

To attempt any of the three options, drive to the Indian Ford junction, 5 miles west of Sisters on U.S. 20. At this junction, travel 4 miles north on FS1139 to the junction with FS1318. It is 7 miles

by road and trail from this junction to the top of Black Butte. The route is well-signed. Proceed as far as possible by car, and, when stopped by snow, commence skiing.

Touring on the lower reaches of the Black Butte Road is primarily flat and suitable for beginning ski tourers. As the road to the top climbs, however, it deteriorates, and the final mile to the actual trailhead is primitive. The remaining 2 miles to the summit would best be done under good conditions by experienced skiers. Because of elevation and exposed south slope, snow conditions above timberline could prove icy.

Round Lake Road—
This road, FS1319, previously mentioned in the Powerline Loop tour, is a suitable addition to that trip for skiers wanting a longer tour. It can be approached directly from U.S. 20 simply by continuing on former FS1317 from the parking area to its eventual junction with FS1319.

From the junction, the distance to Round Lake is 5 miles. Because of an elevation gain of nearly 1,000 feet, tourers are rewarded by an easy glide to the cars.

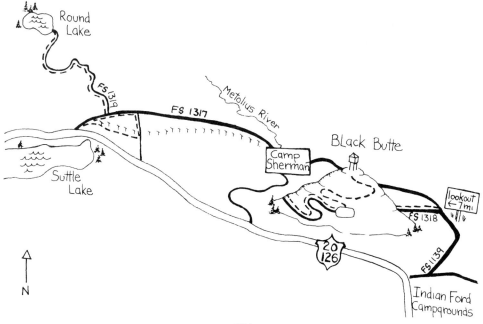

soap creek meadow

Trail tour
8 miles round-trip (from Pole Creek trailhead)
Deschutes National Forest
Sisters Ranger District
Map: Three Sisters Wilderness (free from the Forest Service)

The tour into Soap Creek Meadow, located in the Three Sisters Wilderness Area at the base of the North Sister, is best attempted under two conditions: first, it should be done in the spring, May or June; second, it should be an overnight or multi-day outing.

Primary reasons for these stipulations are the difficulty of the approach and the elevation gain (1700 feet in 4 miles). Pole Creek trailhead, starting point for the tour, lies at 5,300 feet elevation; hence, it is not open until late in the season. Elevation of the meadows is 7,000 feet.

Spring days, as the weather starts to improve, are the best time to visit the meadow. Base camps for climbs of the North and Middle Sisters are often made there, and good touring on the open slopes above timberline and at the foot of glaciers is abundant. From the meadow, the North Sister is directly to the west and climbs of nearby ridges bring many of the peaks along the crest of the Cascades into view.

To reach the area, drive to the town of Sisters, 20 miles north of Bend in Central Oregon. From Sisters, go 1¼ miles west on Oregon 242 and turn south on Forest Service Road 1536. Follow FS 1536 approximately 11 miles to its end at Pole Creek Springs. The route is well-signed and parking space is available at the trailhead, if snow has melted.

From the trailhead, follow Trail 96D 1¼ miles southwest and uphill to its junction with Trail 96. At this junction, turn right and follow Trail 96 for one-half mile as it heads out in a north-westerly direction. At this point, stop, take out map and compass and prepare to go cross-country.

From the jump-off point on Trail 96, Soap Creek Meadow lies at the foot of the North Sister, about 2 miles west with maybe a shade of bearing toward the south. Hopefully, it will be a clear day. Simply aim straight for the North Sister, which is readily visible from most locations except behind ridges. The eastern-most ridge on the North Sister is a piece of rock predominantly yellow-gold in color and highly visible. Head straight for it.

Needless to say, individuals attempting this tour would be advised to carry adequate supplies and a storehouse of knowledge in terms of compass use and cross-country travel. For the independent and prepared tourer, Soap Creek Meadow is a worthwhile objective. It is a cross-country ski tour in the finest sense of the terminology. Enjoy it.

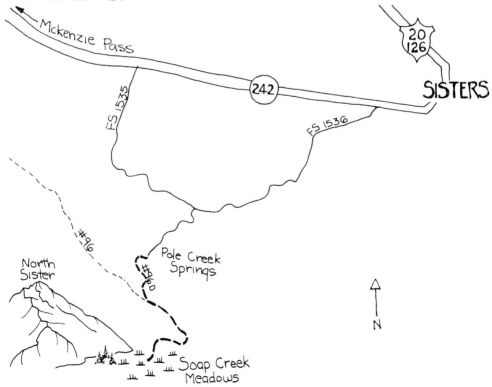

Mckenzie Pass

20
126

FS 1535

242

SISTERS

FS 1536

#96

North Sister

Pole Creek Springs

#96D

N

Soap Creek Meadows

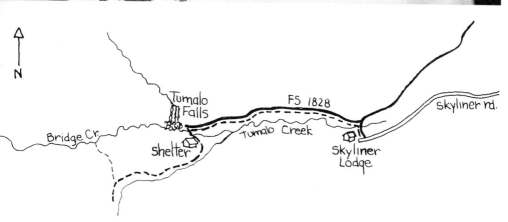

tumalo falls - tumalo shelter

Road and short trail tour
6 miles round-trip
Deschutes National Forest
Bend Ranger District
Map: Broken Top Quadrangle

Visiting Bend and want to give ski touring a try? Looking for a pleasant day tour, moderate in length, scenic in terrain and lacking in difficulty? Head for Tumalo Falls.

Tumalo Falls is located west of Bend and is reached by following signs mentioning Skyliner Road. Skyliner Road parallels Tumalo Creek and is generally plowed to its end at the 10½ mile point.

Closely adjacent to the turn-around at road's end is the old Skyliner Lodge, currently associated with the Bend Chapter of the Oregon Nordic Club. Nordic Club members are often around on winter weekends and can give directions and up-to-the-minute advice concerning local conditions and tours in the area.

To reach Tumalo Falls, park near the end of Skyliner Road; then ski back a short distance and take the first road encountered on the north or left side of the highway which begins the tour with a short sloping run to the bridge crossing Tumalo Creek. At the road junction shortly thereafter, head west on Forest Service Road 1828, paralleling the creek. A sign says Tumalo Falls is 3 miles.

At some points FS1828 will appear to fork. These forks are apparently due to waterline right-of-ways. In any event, by taking left forks and staying parallel to the creek, you can reach the Tumalo Falls campground without difficulty.

The falls, a beautiful sight in a winter setting, can be seen in part from the campground. A better view can be had by following the path to a viewpoint slightly above the campground. One caution: the last portion of the trail to the viewpoint can be extremely icy. Skiers would do well to take off their skis for the last 100 feet and continue cautiously on foot.

An interesting side trip can be made to Tumalo Shelter which is located one-quarter mile southeast of the campground, downstream from the junction of Tumalo Creek and Bridge Creek.

To reach the shelter, cross Tumalo Creek on the bridge entering the campground and turn left, downstream on the south side. The trail follows the south bank and is visible via signs. The shelter is a short distance away, just beyond the point where the trail crosses Bridge Creek on a footbridge and climbs a short hill.

Some wood may be found in the shelter. If so, outdoor etiquette deems that you replace what you use. A small sven-type saw can be carried for this purpose, and extra wood for the next party should be brought in and bucked up before leaving. This is part of the mystique surrounding ski tourers which sets them apart from the common herd. It is a mystique worth maintaining.

tumalo lake road

Road tour
2½ miles round-trip
Deschutes National Forest
Bend Ranger District
Map: Broken Top Quadrangle

Tumalo Lake Road is a good place to go if you have only a short time and wish to get some invigorating exercise. It also has merit for those individuals who wish to perfect downhill or climbing techniques.

Trail length is 2½ miles round-trip. It is woods skiing, no view, through a heavily forested area on narrow, single-lane roads featuring gentle to moderate grades.

To reach Tumalo Lake Road, follow the Skyliner Road west from Bend 10¼ miles until you reach a large, cleared hillside on the south side of the road frequented by ski jumpers, tobogganers, sledders and the like. The road starts slightly west of this area on the south side of the highway. Part of the roadway is sometimes used as a race course for cross-country skiers associated with the Oregon Nordic Club, and use of their track is possible when competition is not in session.

Tumalo Lake Road will not take you to Tumalo Lake. Shortly before arriving there, the road passes onto private land, and a gate plus "No Trespassing" signs indicate further travel is prohibited.

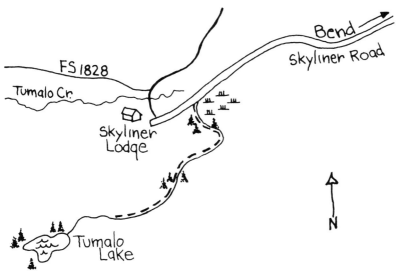

Bend

Skyliner Road

FS 1828

Tumalo Cr.

Skyliner Lodge

Tumalo Lake

N

swampy lakes shelter

Trail tour
4½ miles round-trip
Deschutes National Forest
Bend Ranger District
Maps: Broken Top and Wanoga Butte Quadrangles

Swampy Lakes Shelter, located in the foothills on the east side of the Cascade range, is a popular tour for cross-country skiers in the Bend area.

The shelter, situated slightly north of Swampy Lakes, is 2.3 miles from the Cascades Lakes Highway. The trail climbs gently for 1½ miles, then progresses through slightly rolling country the remaining distance to the shelter. To find the shelter upon reaching Swampy Lakes, ski across the lake on the western end (provided it is frozen), and enter the forest on the northern side. The shelter is a short distance beyond in the trees.

Primary difficulty on this tour is finding the trailhead and following the trail. To find the trailhead, drive 16 miles west of Bend on Oregon 46, the Cascades Lakes Highway. Parking space for the trail is located on the south side of the roadway, one-quarter mile east of the trail's beginning point on the road's north side.

From the plowed turnout, cross the highway and ski west up the north side of the road for one-quarter mile to a spur road which is discernible as a defile in the trees. Ski down this road some 50 yards and look for the beginning of the trail on the west side of the spur road. Depending on snow conditions, a sign may be visible denoting Trail 23, the Swampy Lakes Trail. In addition, some florescent orange markers leading off to the west are tacked to trees.

Approximately 60 yards from the spur road an aluminum trail sign and a second "23" marker may be visible,

depending on snow depth, and are definite indications that you are on the correct route.

From this point, follow blazes, florescent markers and the pruned branches on trees as the trail goes up a draw in a slightly northwesterly direction.

As the route progresses, you will notice a Forest Service road off through the trees to the right which you should parallel for some distance until the trail swings more to the north. Eventually the trail passes over a small ridge and drops down to rolling country, well-signed, for the remainder of the distance to the shelter.

Groups from ski touring organizations in the Bend area annually lay in a supply of winter wood at this shelter. Individuals are welcome to use such wood, but efforts should be made to replace the supply prior to departure. A small axe or light-weight saw is a handy item to carry for this purpose.

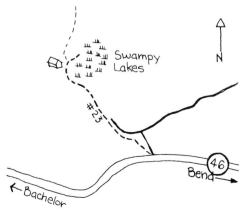

tumalo mountain

Trail and cross-country tour
3 miles round-trip
Deschutes National Forest
Bend Ranger District
Map: Three Sisters Wilderness (free from the Forest Service)

Tumalo Mountain, at 7,775 feet, is one of the higher vantage points in the vicinity of Bachelor Butte, Broken Top and the Three Sisters, and it offers a challenging day tour for advanced skiers with downhill skill, primarily because of an elevation gain of 1300 feet in 1¼ miles.

To get to Tumalo Mountain, follow the Cascades Lakes Highway, Oregon 46, west from Bend as if headed for Mt. Bachelor Ski area. Upon reaching the Dutchman Flat area, 1 mile east of Egan Memorial Lodge, you will encounter a road junction where the ski area access road departs and the Cascades Lakes Highway is blocked by snow. Park at this junction. The summit of Tumalo lies slightly northeast and can be discerned as a tree-covered ridge with open slopes toward the top.

Route to the top is open to the choice of the party. A jeep road, well-covered with snow in winter, winds to the summit 1¾ miles to the east of the junction; however, most parties head directly to the top from the junction itself, relying either on intuition or map and compass. As the crow flies, it is about 1¼ miles to the top, but because of abrupt elevation gain, you should plan 3 to 3½ hours for the climb.

The view from the top features the Three Sisters, Bachelor Butte, Broken Top and a host of other Cascades peaks with the Central Oregon Desert stretching to the east.

Several recommendations: because of the elevation, the summit is often windy; therefore, warm and protective clothing is definitely in order. In addition, abrupt cliffs, rock out-croppings and cornices are hazards on the northeast side of the mountain.

Finally, again because of the wind, you can also encounter hardpack snow and ice patches. Ski tourers without the aid of downhill skill or steel edges should exercise caution on the descent. The upper slopes and the top of the mountain, dotted with small clumps of wind-blown mountain pine and other shrubs, allow long traverses and a gradual descent.

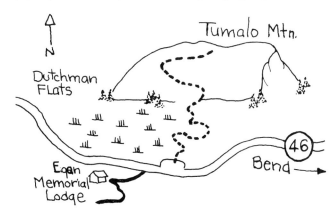

broken top crater

Open country touring
8-10 miles round-trip
Deschutes National Forest
Bend Ranger District
Map: Three Sisters Wilderness
(free from the Forest Service)

Broken Top and Bachelor Butte, two 9,000 foot volcanic peaks in the central Cascades west of Bend, look down on perhaps the most consistently good touring to be had in Oregon. Ski touring at Bachelor is a magnet for tourers from throughout the state.

What is so good about Mt. Bachelor? Primarily it is the elevation and weather. Whereas most accessible areas in the Cascades are in the 4,000-5,000 foot elevation span, touring in the Bachelor-Broken Top area begins at 6,000 feet. Consequently, snow is consistently newer, deeper and colder than most similarly accessible places throughout the state.

The presence of five major volcanic peaks, a scenic asset, is also conducive to continual weather changes. As the mountains generate their own weather, dry powder snowfalls appear with some semblance of regularity.

The terrain is characterized by cinder-flat meadows interspersed with forested sectors, eventually giving way to open slopes above timberline. Roads and trails are basically few, and the tourer's inclination is toward directional touring —i.e., setting an objective and heading out cross-country until you reach it. Peaks abound for orientation (unless weather is socked in), and most people simply take a bearing and go.

Jump-off point for tourers is Dutchman Flat. To get there, travel west of Bend on Oregon 46, the Cascades Lakes Highway, as though headed to Mt. Bachelor Ski Area. At the 22 mile point, you reach the final turn-off to Mt. Bachelor. At this junction the road to the ski

area is plowed and well-signed, while Oregon 46 continues only a short distance farther, being plowed out for 100 yards beyond the junction to accommodate ski tourers and an unhealthy number of snowmobiles.

Snowmobiles, it should be noted, are somewhat obnoxious in the Dutchman Flat area; however, by skirting the fringes in the trees at the base of Tumalo Mountain, you reach the shelter of ridges and as you gain altitude and distance the impact of their presence lessens.

Goals for ski tours in this area are up to the individual. In the area around Todd Lake and beyond, approaching Broken Top Crater, tree-fringed ridges with occasional meadows offer good skiing.

As this is written, studies are being made by local ski touring organizations and the Forest Service toward the idea of plowing the Cascades Lakes Highway farther during the winter months to allow greater access to backcountry areas. The advent of the snowmobile has ended the isolation of these formerly winter-locked areas and the long range capacity of these vehicles has created a demand for territory. Indirectly, this may benefit ski tourers.

If the road were kept open from Bend to Highway 58, a multitude of previously inaccessible country would open to ski touring use. Such tours, off limits to snowmobiles due to terrain or presently existing motor vehicle closures are now virtually out of reach save only to people willing to approach them via trips of several days duration.

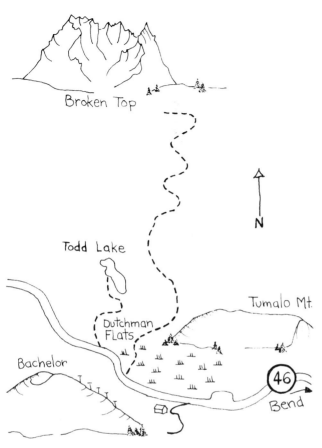

Broken Top

Todd Lake

Dutchman Flats

Bachelor

Tumalo Mt.

N

(46)

Bend

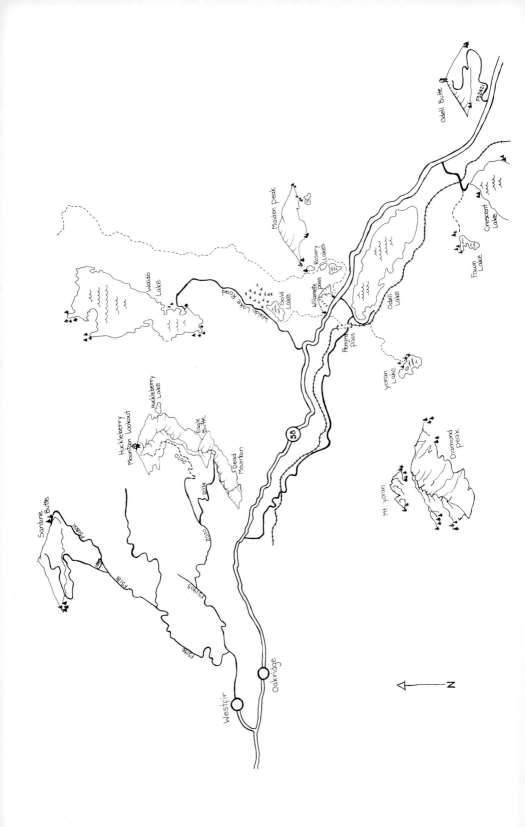

williamette pass tours

Ski tourers often overlook Willamette Pass as a potentially desirable touring site because of notions that snow is somehow wetter or that challenging terrain is virtually non-existent. This just is not true.

Many desirable touring destinations are located within a short distance of Willamette Pass's 5,126 foot summit. The possibilities range from a delightfully easy beginner's tour into Gold Lake featuring problem-free terrain to more complex runs traversing the interior of the Diamond Peak Wilderness Area. There is something for everyone.

In addition, a number of other tours, located both east and west of the pass, are included in this section. All have a basically common theme: they are road tours to the tops of scenic promontories, in most cases the sites of Forest Service Lookout Stations. Sardine Butte, Huckleberry Mountain, Odell Butte, Walker Mountain—all offer the simplicity of a road tour but also feature amazingly speedy shortcuts.

Trips to places of this nature, in view of this publication, are perhaps the plus-factor in a sport which is growing in popularity with every year. These are the tours which will never be crowded. They won't be crowded for two reasons: one, most people methodically drive to the traditional summit touring sites, week after week. Secondly, even if people do start touring to the unknown buttes or mountains, there is enough territory to absorb them. On the western and eastern slopes of the Cascades exist an incredible band of peaks and ridges at moderate elevation loosely termed the "lesser peaks." They range from 3,000 to 7,000 feet in elevation. During the summer months these areas add to Oregon's economy in that they are the prime producers of timber. Once you become fairly familiar with any given area—its roads, ridges and clearcuts—the possibilities for incredible ski tours become more and more obvious. The cut-over land shunned in summer for the pristine beauty of the high alpine wilderness, is redeemed each autumn with a blanket of white.

In addition to these tours which are off the beaten path, a number of other tours in the Willamette Pass vicinity are unique. They offer options in terms of length, route traveled and destination. A trip to Gold Lake, for example, can be simply in and out on the same track or, with a car shuttle, can end farther west and downhill via the Waldo Lake Road.

As with most tours in the book, those centered on Willamette Pass are cited primarily to give people new to the area or new to the sport a chance to familiarize themselves with available resources. Once you determine the lay of the land, the only governing factor in selecting new ski tours is your desire and ambition.

sardine butte

Road tour
10 miles round-trip (when possible)
Willamette National Forest
Oakridge Ranger District
Map: Sardine Butte Quadrangle and
**   Oakridge R.D. Fireman's Map**

"I've been touring out to Sardine Butte," the man said, smiling smugly. "Sardine where?" ask 99 percent of the resident tourers, scratching their heads. "You know, Sardine Butte—up there, east of Sinker Mountain, west of Hiyu Ridge, a hop, skip and jump from the Ironside Mine."
"Oh!"

Never heard of it? Few people have. Sardine Butte is merely another example of the incredible, positively unbelievable ski tours currently existing, out there, uncharted, in the booming vastness of our Oregon Cascades.

Sardine Butte is off the beaten path. It lies some 25-30 miles northeast of Oakridge, on the divide overlooking the Lowell, Blue River and Oakridge ranger districts of the Willamette National Forest. There is a road to the mountain's 5,214 foot summit, the site of a former Forest Service lookout. The view features peaks ranging the length of the Cascades.

Sardine Butte is a good place to go. For 5 miles of uphill skiing, the tourer is rewarded with a return run back to the bottom which drops 1600 feet in elevation. In addition, because of a number of clearcuts, open slopes are available and steep shortcuts for those individuals with downhill skills, offer un-tracked, virgin slopes when snow depth is sufficient to hide stumps and bushes.

To get to Sardine Butte, drive east of Eugene on Oregon 58 some 37 miles to Westfir, a lumber community northwest of Oakridge. At the central, stop-sign controlled intersection adjacent to a large, green, covered bridge spanning the Willamette River, proceed north along a gravel road which passes through the lumber yard. This road eventually emerges as a paved highway, Forest Service Road 196.

Follow FS196 13½ miles, while paralleling the north fork of the Middle Fork of the Willamette River, to the junction of FS196 and FS181. Follow FS181 some 3 miles to the junction of FS181 and FS18011.

At this junction you must make a choice. Depending on snow conditions, either fork may be appropriate. Road FS181 is the eventual ski route, but because of lumbering activity and conditions of sun and shade FS18011 may be clear of snow earlier, permitting the party to drive to a higher elevation. In any event, drive as high as possible.

Between 5 and 6 miles from the junction of FS181 and FS18011, a short connecting road, known either as FS 1884 or simply spur "A," ties in between FS181 and FS18011. Drive or ski on this connecting spur to FS181. The distance to the top of Sardine Butte from this junction is 5 miles.

The tour is basically a road tour; however, a number of large clearcuts permit variations which may appeal to the adventuresome individual. By traversing, studying maps and cutting across appropriate clearcuts, both going up and returning, you can save considerable mileage.

This tour is best attempted either early in the season with the first snows or late in the year when the warm days of spring melt snow at lower elevations.

Sardine Butte, as a ski tour, represents one of the essential joys of the activity: its diversity. Spring does not herald the retiring of skis until the first storms of next winter; rather, it is a time of new exploration—a chance to visit areas previously inaccessible. Many such tours are out there, they have only to be found.

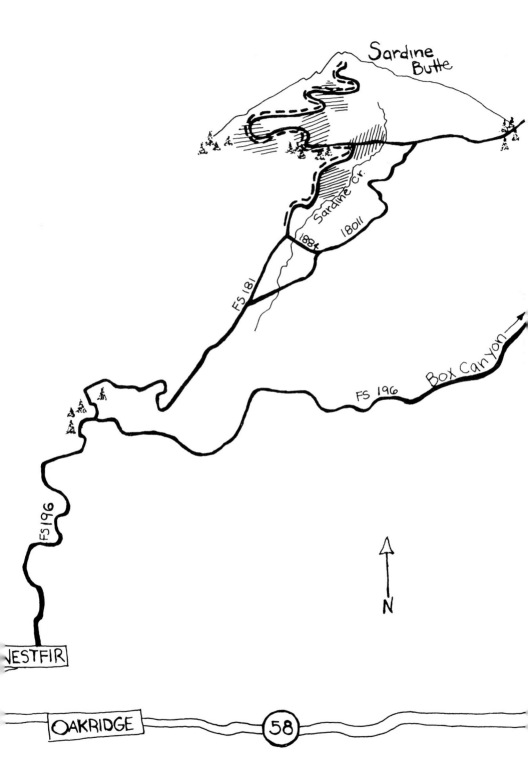

Sardine Butte

Sardine Cr.

1801l

1884

FS 181

Box Canyon

FS 196

FS 196

N

WESTFIR

OAKRIDGE   58

huckleberry mountain

Road tour
6-15 miles round-trip
Willamette National Forest
Oakridge Ranger District
Map: Sardine Butte Quadrangle and
Oakridge R.D. Fireman's Map

Huckleberry Mountain, rising to a height of 5,549 feet, offers a fine view of the high country east of Oakridge on a clear day. It is a tour for experienced tourers and is variable in length, depending, as always, on snow conditions and the time of year attempted. The best months, generally, are March and April, when the snow pack has stabilized.

As with many tours located off all-weather routes, the status of low-elevation secondary roads often is the critical factor in determining whether or not a tour to out-of-the-way places is possible. Huckleberry Mountain is in this category. A call to local authorities on the Oakridge Ranger District of the Willamette National Forest is often helpful in determining conditions prior to a trip.

To get to Huckleberry Mountain, travel east of Eugene on Oregon 58, taking the turn-off just short of Oakridge leading to the community of Westfir. From Westfir, follow the High Prairie Road for 9 miles until it leaves private land and enters the National Forest and becomes Forest Service Road 1905.

Follow FS1905 until it forks and FS2070 heads to the east. Follow FS2070 for 1 mile to a second fork and bear left. Continue on this fork an additional 1½ miles, at which point you will encounter a final fork. Again, take the left fork. Huckleberry Mountain Lookout is 4½ miles from this junction.

The tour up the road to the lookout passes through numerous clearcuts and if snow is abundant, road cuts may be filled and in some cases, obscured. Numerous shortcuts can also be taken, depending on the willingness of party members to veer off the road and ascend steep slopes. Since the current U.S. Geological Survey quadrangle for the area was mapped in 1956, an up-to-date Forest Service Fireman's Map is desirable in order to plot accurate progress throughout this tour.

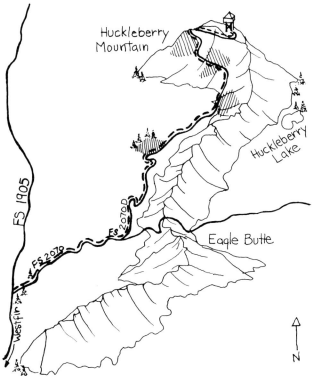

Huckleberry Mountain

Huckleberry Lake

FS 1905

FS 2070D

FS 2070

Eagle Butte

Westfir

N

dead mountain

Road tour
4 miles round-trip
Willamette National Forest
Oakridge Ranger District
Map: Sardine Butte Quadrangle and
Oakridge R.D. Fireman's Map

Looking for a novel tour? Something out of the ordinary? Tired of winding up the same roads to the same trails on the same mountain passes? Then take a whirl out to Dead Mountain.

A short tour, 2 miles one-way, the route is best done during those times of snowfall at lower elevations. The only problem to encounter is elevation. The road climbs.

The situation is thus: From the jump-off point, tour in approximately 1 mile, then spend the second mile in a medium-arduous altitude-gaining climb, at the end of which you arrive at a ridgetop and the Dead Mountain Divide. Actually, Dead Mountain lies more to the southwest, and a road leads out along the ridgeline from the pass area and takes the tourer out over promontories which offer views of the 1967 Dead Mountain Fire.

To get to Dead Mountain, travel east of Eugene on Oregon 58 and take the turn-off just short of Oakridge leading to the community of Westfir. Follow the High Prairie Road northeast from Westfir until it leaves private land and becomes Forest Service Road 1905, approximately 9 miles from Westfir.

Depending on snow conditions, follow FS1905 to its junction with FS2070. Park at this junction. The tour commences at this point, goes 1 mile up FS2070 to the next junction, then continues on the right fork FS2070A. Road FS2070A peaks out at the Dead Mountain Divide and offers a brisk run back to the cars for frustrated downhillers, if the snow is right.

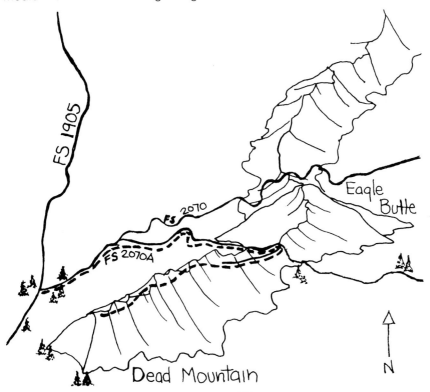

gold lake

Road and lake touring
4 miles round-trip
Willamette National Forest
Oakridge Ranger District
Map: Waldo Lake Quadrangle

For individuals attempting ski touring for the first time, Gold Lake and the road approaching it offer perhaps the best first-time ski tour in the vicinity of Willamette Pass, if not in the entire central Cascades.

Distance to Gold Lake is approximately 2 miles. The trail, a narrow gravel road in summer, winds through large timber for its entire length. The road is level, though there is a slight drop in elevation as the lake is neared.

Gold Lake is an ideal tour for neophytes because it offers more than the simple mechanics of learning technique or skiing around in circles. It is a legitimate tour but without the problems associated with more rigorous routes. Primarily, there is a destination, a route and a view. Little more is needed.

The Gold Lake road features flat sections and gentle slopes offering easy running, once a good track has been set. Upon reaching the lake, the road crosses the outlet on a substantial wooden bridge and a three-sided Forest Service shelter overlooks the meandering outlet channel, a good spot for lunch or overnight camping.

Because of thin ice, the area around the bridge is not usually a safe place to ski onto the lake and you should make definite checks on ice thickness and stability before venturing out.

By following the road across the bridge and around the lake you can cut down to the shoreline on the western side where the ice is usually firmer. In addition to the outlet, two other potential soft spots occur where streams enter the lake at the northwest and northern

edges. Such areas are usually visible and can be avoided.

The best place for sun and a good view of nearby Diamond Peak is at the edge of the Gold Lake Bog Research Natural Area at the northern-most end of the lake. A meandering creek traverses the open bog and the mountain rises to the south above the lake and a fringe of trees.

To reach Gold Lake, travel east of Oakridge toward Willamette Pass on Oregon 58. After arriving at the Waldo Lake cut-off, continue east 2¼ miles on Oregon 58, until you reach a small sign reading "Gold Lake" and pointing north. Ample parking should be available on both sides of the highway. The Gold Lake road, Forest Service 223, begins on the north side of the highway. The whole interchange is one-half mile west of Willamette Pass summit, so if you reach the downhill ski area and have not found it, turn around and retrace your steps.

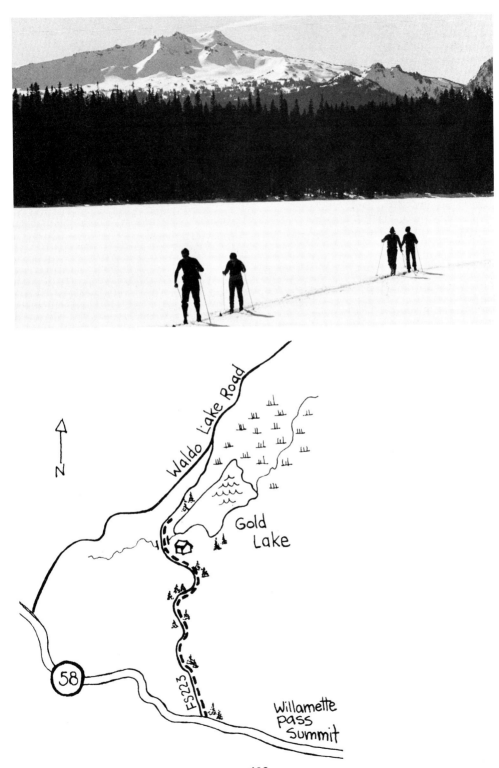

pengra pass loops

Road tour
Willamette National Forest
4, 3 or 6 miles average
    (depending on route or shuttles)
Oakridge Ranger District
Map: Waldo Lake Quadrangle

Pengra Pass, a second and little known route crossing the divide between Lane and Klamath counties near Odell Lake, is suitable for tourers looking for an unobstructed road tour or some open slopes for downhill touring.

To get to Pengra Pass, drive east of Oakridge on Oregon 58 to the Gold Lake junction, one-half mile west of Willamette Pass Ski Area. Two turnouts are customarily plowed at the junction: one on the north side of the highway for the Gold Lake Road and the other on the south side for the route to Pengra Pass, Forest Service Road 2329.

From the junction, ski southwest 1¼ miles down virtually flat road to Pengra Pass. A yellow and black snow marker announces your arrival. At this point you may chose to:

1.) Turn east on a brief but enjoyable one-half mile ski down moderately steep road to railroad tracks and the Odell Lake Road a short distance beyond. The lake is a bit farther through the trees. The road, usually plowed out around the west end of the lake, can be skied on the road shoulders or walked up. Once you reach the highway, walk or hitchhike 1 mile west to the Gold Lake junction.

2.) Turn west at the snow marker. Recent logging in the vicinity has created a maze of skid-roads, clearcut areas, and, when the snow is deep, light and powdery, some amazingly good downhill skiing. Untracked slopes. No lines. No lift tickets. You can hike to the top to your heart's content or continue down the road and discover more untracked territory. Following a day's play, return to Pengra Pass, then either turn east or return to the junction by your original track.

3.) Take a third route which is a bit longer. It involves skiing an additional 5 miles beyond Pengra Pass, west and downhill, crossing the Southern Pacific railroad tracks and eventually coming out on Oregon 58 a short distance above Salt Creek Falls Campground. Elevation drop is 850 feet.

A vehicle should be left at the lower end of the run on the way to the junction. To find the ending point, watch for Salt Creek Falls, just east of the highway tunnel. One-quarter mile past the major viewpoint turnout a new spur road veers

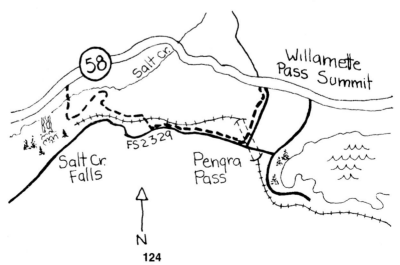

off Oregon 58 on the south side, slightly west of FS 2204. Leave a vehicle here.

Basic instructions are the same for the tour's first mile. Beyond this point, begin watching the west or right side of the road for a spur road running down to the west. Several likely looking openings exist, but the primary clue is telephone line insulators which are still mounted in trees along the roadway for most of the route. If you reach Pengra Pass and haven't found them, backtrack.

Follow the road paralleling the insulators. This runs west, downhill and flat, for 2¼ miles, until the road comes out of the timber on the south side of the Southern Pacific railroad tracks. Two cautions: once you reach the tracks the tendency is to ski along its southern edge for some distance, looking for a place to descend a slight embankment, prior to crossing. Deer Creek, a fairly large stream, passes under the tracks near this point and is often hard to discern until you are almost upon it. Corniced banks are a some-time hazard.

The other caution is fairly logical — watch out for trains.

Once on the north side of the tracks, ski west around a curve until a large metal signalling device spanning the tracks comes into view. Watch to the right again for the road and phone insulators which begin before you reach the signalling tower. The road, below the level of the tracks, drops into the canyon and eventually forks a short distance farther. At this junction bear right, leaving the insulators, down a steeper road which s-curves and finally intersects a third thoroughfare. Continue west downhill.

This road is of recent construction and is not shown on current maps. Some selective-cut logging has gone on in the area, and the road continues down the canyon eventually crossing Salt Creek on a new bridge before rejoining Oregon 58 and the awaiting shuttle car.

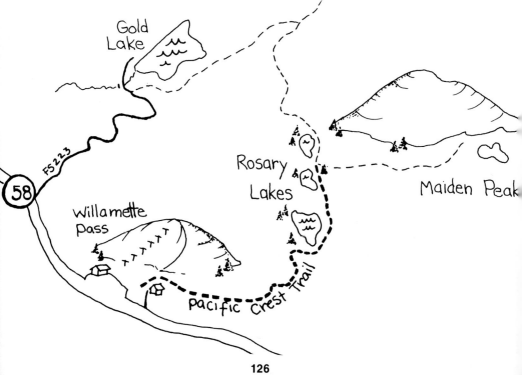

rosary lakes

Trail tour
6 miles round-trip
Deschutes National Forest
Crescent Ranger District
Map: Waldo Lake and Odell Lake Quadrangles

The Rosary Lakes, located northeast of Willamette Pass on the Pacific Crest Trail, are a reasonable objective for a moderately easy day tour. Depending on certain variables, the trail can be suitable for neophytes with downhill skills or some ski touring experience. Variables include such items as snow condition, time of the year and the ability to remain on the Pacific Crest Trail.

The final variable is perhaps the most crucial as far as beginning skiers are concerned. When you can follow it, the Pacific Crest is a relatively gentle 3 miles of skiing into Lower Rosary Lake.

Basically, the trail heads almost due east for the first 2 miles from the trailhead near the eastern boundary of Willamette Pass Ski Area. At 2½ miles the trail swings north and finding it can become a problem. A tendency for tourers is to traverse high, around a ridge, which can lead to steep and often icy terrain. In reality, the trail tends to skirt the ridge at a lower elevation on gentle slopes, prior to the last 200 yards and a brief climb up a short hill to a bench-like basin in which the lake sits.

To get to the Rosary Lakes trailhead, drive east from Eugene on Oregon 58 to Willamette Pass. Upon reaching Willamette Pass summit, continue east on Oregon 58 past the parking area for several hundred feet and turn north on a short, plowed gravel road leading to a gravel storage shed owned by the State Highway Department. The trail parallels the shed on the north side in the trees and some parking is available near the structure, though care should be taken not to block access to the entrance as snow-removal equipment need room to turn around and pick up their loads.

Trail signs are usually visible northwest of the plowed area at the edge of the trees. It is also a short ski from the trailhead to Willamette Pass Ski Area and if a large party is planning to make the tour, it might be advisable to park in the ski area's parking lot.

Two smaller lakes lie north of Lower Rosary and can be sought by the more ambitious party members. In addition, possibilities for longer tours include a loop down to Gold Lake via Douglas Horse Pasture or a ski mountaineering ascent of Maiden Peak.

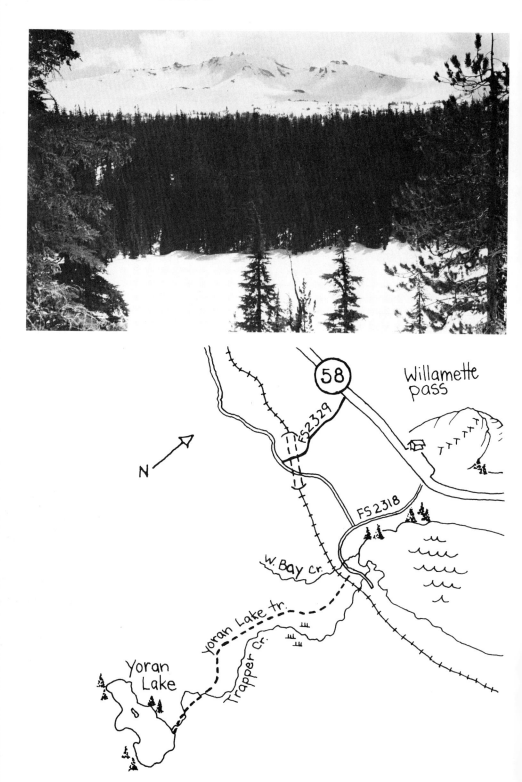

N

58

Willamette
Pass

FS2329

FS 2318

W. Bay cr.

Yoran Lake tr.

Trapper cr.

Yoran
Lake

yoran lake

Trail tour
8 miles round-trip
Deschutes National Forest
Crescent Ranger District
Map: Waldo Lake Quadrangle

Looking for a real wilderness challenge? Try following the Yoran Lake trail in April, May or June. That is assuming you can even find the trailhead. For a day tour, Yoran Lake is an arduous trip, but worth it.

Yoran Lake lies at the foot of Diamond Peak, well within the boundaries of the Diamond Peak Wilderness Area. Trail length is roughly 4 miles one way, but late in the year, particularly in a year of heavy snows, finding the trail is difficult and following it nearly impossible. Definite requirements for the trip are U.S. Geological Survey Topographic map, a compass and a general feeling for the lay of the land and prominent local landmarks such as Odell Lake, Lakeview Mountain, Diamond Peak and the open slopes at Willamette Pass Ski Area.

To begin the tour, drive to Willamette Pass, 65 miles east of Eugene on Oregon 58. One-quarter mile east of the summit, turn south on Forest Service Road 2318. Depending on snow conditions, this road may or may not be open. It is plowed sporadically throughout the winter, seemingly on whim, and winds down to a series of summer homes and resort facilities along the western shore of Odell Lake.

In any event, from the junction of FS 2318 and Oregon 58, proceed approximately 2 miles, either by car or ski, until you arrive at West Bay Creek, which is signed. The Yoran Lake Trail meets FS2318 several yards south of the creek and parallels the creek for the first mile until reaching the creek's source, a small lake.

The most notable obstacle in following the trail is a number of very definite bench-like ridges lying perpendicular to it. Though the trail is known to traverse such slopes via the map, visible proof of this circumstance is in short supply.

Three possibilities exist for finding Yoran Lake if the trail is not visible: 1.) Take a compass course starting at the junction of West Bay Creek and FS2318. 2.) At all times stay north of Trapper Creek. Follow the north fork of Trapper Creek to its source, a three-fingered lake northeast of Yoran Lake. 3.) If you get too far north of Trapper Creek, you will come upon a number of small lakes and by ascertaining their shapes and approximate places on the map, you can then determine your location.

After a bit of wandering, all lakes begin to look like the Genuine Item; however, Yoran Lake is far and away the largest in the vicinity and can be noted by a parapet-like ridge along its eastern shore and an island with approximately 20 trees near its northern end.

Once you have arrived at Yoran Lake, a good route out if your trail was less than direct, is to follow the outlet from the southeast edge of Yoran Lake down to its intersection with the north fork of Trapper Creek. You can follow Trapper Creek back to Odell Lake, or, perhaps more ideally, to a large open swamp area near the head of West Bay Creek where you can intersect the Yoran Lake Trail.

Yoran Lake is an excellent site for an overnight ski tour, or for those people planning a winter climb of Diamond Peak or Mt. Yoran. You can see both peaks from the lake and can visually plot an appropriate route to their lower reaches.

fawn lake

Road and trail tour
6 miles round-trip
Deschutes National Forest
Crescent Ranger District
Maps: Odell Lake and Waldo Lake
Quadrangles

Fawn Lake, a sizeable body of water just outside the eastern boundary of the Diamond Peak Wilderness Area, offers fine views of Redtop and Lakeview mountains and is for individuals who want a combination of trail and road touring.

Tour length is 6 miles round-trip.

Drive to the Crescent Lake junction on Oregon 58, 8 miles east of Willamette

Pass. At the junction, graced by a store, restaurant and gas station, an all-weather road turns southwest and leads to the resort community of Crescent Lake, which is also noted as an important switching spot for Southern Pacific Railroad crews on the line between Eugene and Klamath Falls.

The road travels 2 miles from Oregon 58 before crossing the railroad tracks, makes a sharp turn to the southeast and continues 200 yards to the Southern Pacific buildings. The important thing to remember is the railroad crossing. Parking space is usually available on either side of the tracks.

The road to Fawn Lake begins on the west side of the tracks, where the Crescent Lake access road turns sharply in a southeasterly direction. The route goes northwest from this point and a Forest Service "birdback" signboard marks the trail's beginning.

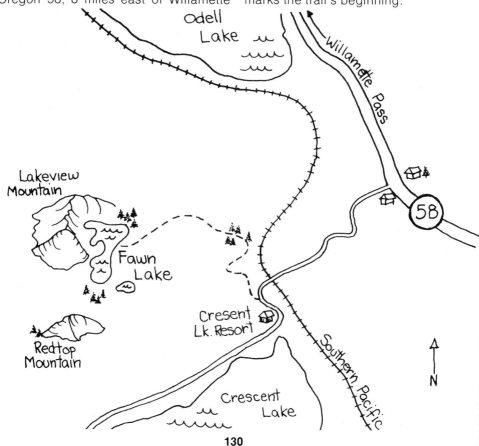

The road, readily discernible as it rolls through the jackpine, passes a small outbuilding after one-quarter mile and continues to a clearing one-half mile farther. It ends in the clearing at the base of a moderately steep ridge, facing an open swath of terrain ascending to the ridgetop, as though for a powerline right-of-way. Facing the swath from the bottom, you will find the trail to Fawn Lake begins in the fringe of trees on the right or north side of the clearing. Another trail also takes off to the left on the south side of the swath. It eventually intersects an access road to campgrounds at nearby Crescent Lake.

For the first three-quarters of a mile, the trail rises gently and heads almost due north. It then swings west, climbing and winding over a series of small hills and benches, and eventually emerges on a small ridge on the east side of Fawn Lake.

As winter snows progress, it may become difficult to follow the trail in its upper reaches. If the route appears hopelessly lost, ski to a vantage point and look for Lakeview Mountain, a rocky, treeless promontory northwest of Fawn Lake. A lower, more symetrical and tree-clad peak lies south of Lakeview Mountain, and by using these two points for orientation and skiing in their direction, you will find Fawn Lake.

While Fawn Lake is an ideal day tour, an overnight trip to the area would allow greater exploration. Forays toward Stag, Saddle or Pretty lakes are possibilities and you could accomplish a loop tour by following the Crater Butte Trail, No. 44, northeast for 4½ miles to Odell Lake Resort.

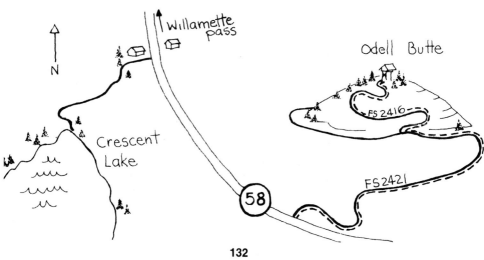

odell butte

Road tour
6-12 miles round-trip
Deschutes National Forest
Crescent Ranger District
Map: Crescent Ranger
District U.S. F.S.

Odell Butte, a volcanic cinder cone a few miles east of Willamette Pass, is a superb destination if you want an invigorating climb with a nice run coming out. At 7,033 feet elevation, the summit offers a view extending from Mt. Scott near Crater Lake north to Mt. Jefferson, with Diamond Peak shimmering above the high Cascade mountain lakes a few miles to the west.

Maximum tour length for Odell Butte is 6 miles one-way. Late in the spring as the sun shines with more regularity and the bulldozers push upward, this distance shortens.

Bulldozers? Yes, bulldozers. A nearby railroad has a communications relay installation on the mountain in addition to a Forest Service lookout station, and the machinery must be serviced throughout the winter. During the harsh months, technicians apparently use sno-cats and snowshoes, but as spring approaches attempts are made to clear the road. These attempts are often thwarted by late storms, and skiable snow usually remains on the shoulders even after the initial cut has been pushed through.

To get to Odell Butte, you must orient from the service station complex east of Willamette Pass on Oregon 58 at the Crescent Lake turn-off. From the turn-off, drive 6½ miles east on Oregon 58 to its junction with Forest Service Road 2421. Depending on snow conditions, the car can be left at this junction or can be driven on FS2421 until the road is impassible.

The primary touring route up Odell Butte begins on FS2421 at Oregon 58. Follow FS2421 for 2 miles to a junction with a spur road veering sharply to the left or west. Follow the spur for one-half mile to its intersection with FS2416. The route switchbacks to the right at this point and follows FS2416 the remainder of the distance to the summit.

Touring up Odell Butte is easy for most of the distance until a sharp switchback on the north side denotes the last one-half mile. The road is noticeably steeper from this point on, and there are two more switchbacks to encounter before reaching the top.

In late spring, snow may have vanished on the last switchback, a well-exposed corner on the warmer south slope. Skis may be left here or carried across bare spots to higher snowbanks. The Forest Service lookout station is 150 yards from this junction. The upper portion of the tower is closed to visitors but the view from its stairway spans the length of the Cascades.

walker mountain

Road tour
6-16 miles round-trip
Deschutes National Forest
Crescent Ranger District
Map: Crescent R.D. Fireman's Map

Walker Mountain, a 7,078 foot peak overlooking the junction of U.S. 97 and Oregon 58 south of Bend and east of Willamette Pass, is a tour best made in early winter or late spring. From its summit, the pine trees spread out below for many miles and the view ranges from Three Sisters south to Mt. McLoughlin.

The main problem with Walker Mountain is the approach. In mid-winter with heavy snows, the starting point from the edge of U.S. 97 would be a round-trip distance of 16 miles. In the spring, however, because of the efforts of the sun and the road-clearing tendencies of lumbermen at lower elevations, it is often possible to drive to the 4 mile point or closer, making the tour to the top much more attractive.

While approaching roads to the mountain are broad and made of gravel, the final 4 miles is much narrower and with a dirt base. The elevation gain is gentle and while there are no severely steep sections, the gentle rise is not so gentle as to hinder an easy slide back to the car once you set a track.

A number of buildings, some visible from the highway below, occupy the mountain's long, ridge-like summit. One, a Forest Service lookout tower, offers an excellent view of the surroundings from mid-way up the tower's stairs. The other building and towers are part of a microwave station.

To get to Walker Mountain, travel to the junction of Oregon 58 and U.S. 97, 92 miles east of Eugene. At the junction turn south on 97 and travel 3 and 6/10 miles to the junction of 97 and Forest Service Road 2628. A sign pointing east reads: "Walker Mountain 8 Miles."

Depending on conditions, follow FS 2628 as far as possible to its junction with FS 2651, which is 4 miles from Walker Mountain's summit. Once on FS 2651, drive as far as you can go, then park and begin skiing.

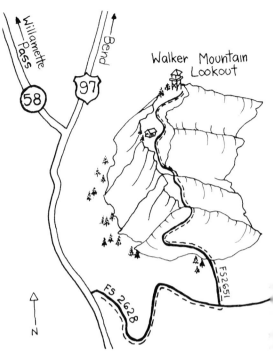

Walker Mountain
Lookout

Willamette
Pass

Bend

58

97

N

FS 2628

FS 2651

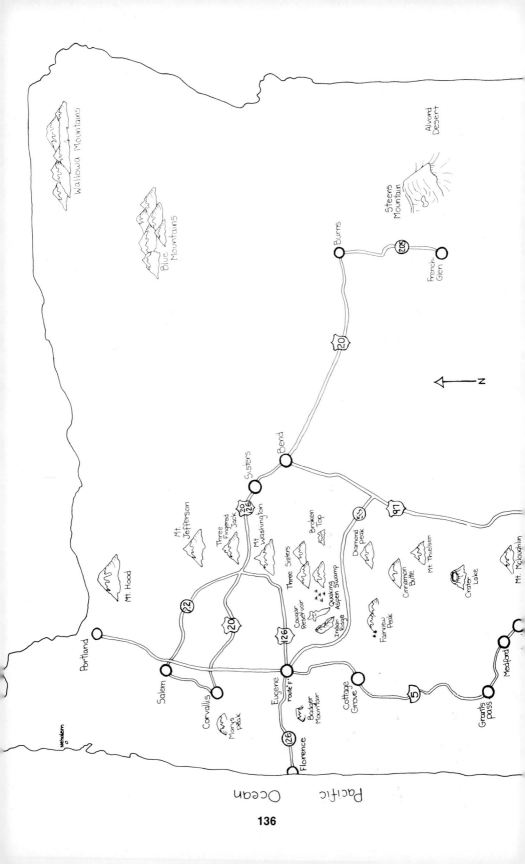

Pacific Ocean

136

bonus tours

Bonus Tours are those ski tours that for one reason or another will not fit neatly into the categories prescribed for other tours in this book. The bonus tours are like people: they have their gleaming good qualities, but in each one there is a flaw.

In ski tours, flaws come in varieties. "Lack of snow during most of winter" is perhaps the most serious. "Inaccessible" and/or "Too far to drive" run a close second. In reality, most bonus tours offer honest, good skiing if you can determine that snow has, indeed, fallen in their localities, and then take the time to get there.

Problems of approach and distance render certain tours into the bonus tour category. Such tours as those to Steens Mountain or Crater Lake are usually more than a weekend's journey and are best tried in several days.

Other tours are included because they occur in unusual places: areas that have snow most of the winter but which the majority of the population has yet to associate with skiing. Such trips as Marys Peak or Indian Ridge are examples. People know the foothills of the Cascades are clogged with snow every year, but no one has thought to ski there.

Actually, bonus tours are representative of the whole adventuresome spirit which has traditionally set ski tourers apart from others. Tourers have long been noted for their independence, self-reliance and ability to make their own way through hill and forest without predetermined paths, guides or directional arrows. This philosophy should not die. It is the very meat and substance of the activity.

To collect your dividends in the bonus tour arena, be on the alert for potential ski touring sites. If you go hiking during the summer or fall months, mentally evaluate each trail as a possible ski tour. Figure access, probable snow depth and the ease with which it could be followed. Is it blazed and are limbs pruned off a considerable distance up the tree trunks? How would it be to ski the same route?

In a nutshell, there is no magic recipe for selecting such ski tours. It is simply a matter of evaluating the existing information, selecting the proper maps and equipment and giving the tour a try. All tours in this publication were done simply on the basis that they looked good. Other than that there were few indications that the tour would bear fruit.

marys peak

Road tour
4-10 miles round-trip
Siuslaw National Forest
Alsea Ranger District
Map: Marys Peak and Alsea
      Quadrangles

Marys Peak, at 4,097 feet, reportedly the highest point in the central Coast Range, is the best tour to take when a change from the Cascades drives you in pursuit of untried territory. It is also good for nearby Willamette Valley residents who wish a brief fling on the skis for a few hours before dinner.

Except during periods of heavy snow, Marys Peak can be approached year-round on a Forest Service access road. You can gain considerable altitude before persistent snow drifts finally block vehicular travel. Depending on the amount of snow and where it occurs, tour length is variable.

In any event, to make the tour drive west of Corvallis to Philomath and pick up Oregon 34 on its way down the Alsea River to Waldport. From Philomath, follow Oregon 34 for 9 miles to its junction with Forest Service Road 1244, the Marys Peak Road. This road is 10 miles long. Because of a southern exposure during most of its climb from Oregon 34, major drifts do not occur until the road swings around to the north side of the mountain, 2 miles from the top near a microwave relay station. If you park near the relay station, two routes to the summit are possible.

The first follows the road to the summit lookout station. The second involves following the road until it leaves the trees, then, when the meadows open up, leaving the road for a more direct route.

The final one-half mile of road to the summit traverses the east slope and then swings around to the southwest. Because of a band of rock bluffs midway up the last meadow, it may be appropriate to return to the road.

From the summit of Marys Peak you can see the coast range to the north, south and west, while the Willamette Valley and the distant peaks of the Cascades are visible to the east. The major summits, from Mt. Hood to Diamond Peak, are readily apparent on a clear day.

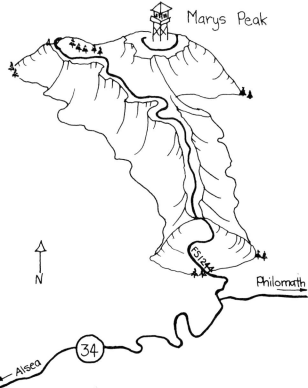

Marys Peak

FS 1244

Philomath

N

34

Alsea

badger mountain

Road tour
4 miles round-trip
International Paper Co./Bureau of Land Management Coast Range
Map: Blachly Quadrangle

A lot of people drive by Badger Mountain every day and don't realize its potential. But who would think about ski touring on the way to the beach?

Badger Mountain lies almost due west of Eugene, slightly south of Route "F", Oregon 126, the main east-west highway between Eugene and Florence. To get there, drive west of Eugene on Oregon 126 to the community of Noti. Cougar Pass, jump-off point for Badger Mountain, is approximately 6 miles west of Noti. Simply follow the mileposts. When you reach Milepost 36, stop. You are now at Cougar Pass. Ample parking is available and the trail, actually a narrow road, begins on the south side of the pass.

Since the route passes over private ground of the International Paper Co., it may be advisable to seek permission to enter. The summit of Badger Mountain, complete with an old fire lookout, is 2 miles from Cougar Pass. The road is fairly flat for the first one-quarter mile, then climbs with increased steepness. Coming out in a good track, you can make long glides for three-quarters of the total distance.

Badger Mountain is excellent for those days when heavy snow blankets the lower elevations. It is a pleasant break from the long drives east to the traditional Cascade touring places. If you decide to go, remember that snow is only a "sometime" commodity in the coastal mountains and weather reports should be checked to determine freezing level. Road reports are also handy, and if the State Police advise: " . . . Chains are required, Eugene to Florence . . . " chances are fairly good that a touring trip to Badger Mountain would be successful.

indian ridge

Road tour
7-20 miles round-trip
Willamette National Forest
Blue River Ranger District
Map: Blue River R.D. Fireman's Map

Not many people have heard of Indian Ridge, but they are familiar with French Pete Valley. Indian Ridge sits west and a little south of French Pete and looks right down into it. The view from the top also features the Three Sisters and other major peaks of the Cascade crest.

A ski tour to Indian Ridge and the lookout station which occupies the summit is best made in the spring when weather is good and snow has receded from the lower elevation access roads. In mid-winter, unless loggers are working in the vicinity and have plowed key roads, chances of getting within 10 miles of the top are slim.

To reach the push-off point for Indian Ridge, drive east of Eugene on U.S. 126 to Blue River. From there, continue 5 miles east on U.S. 126 and turn south on Forest Service Road 163, the access road to Cougar Reservoir and the South Fork of the McKenzie River. Follow FS163 around the reservoir on the west side, then cross the South Fork of the McKenzie as it empties into the reservoir. Continue south on FS163 and parallel the river until you cross French Pete Creek. From the creek, travel one-half mile to the junction with FS1803. This is the final road to Indian Ridge.

Cross the South Fork of the McKenzie and drive on FS1803 as far as possible. From the bridge, distance to Indian Ridge Lookout is 10 miles.

An up-to-date fireman's or multiple use map is especially handy at this point and you should acquire one prior to making the trip. FS1803 winds for 10 miles through an area of very intensive logging and innumerable spur roads can be very misleading. Such a map shows virtually all roads and clearcuts in the area and is much handier than a contour map. Actually, by using both map types, it is possible to plot a shorter course by skiing across clearcuts and cutting switchbacks. It also makes for a speedier descent on the return.

In late April and early May, it is often possible to drive to within 3½ miles of the summit until the lay of the land changes to such an extent that shade is predominant and the upper slopes remain snowed-in. The last 3 miles of road switchbacks up the east slope and then circles around the north end, finally approaching the lookout tower from the southwest side.

The top of Indian Ridge is a flat plateau, grassy in summer. It is almost level the last 150 yards to the lookout. Because of steep cliffs on some sides of the ridge-top, you should take care when approaching edges.

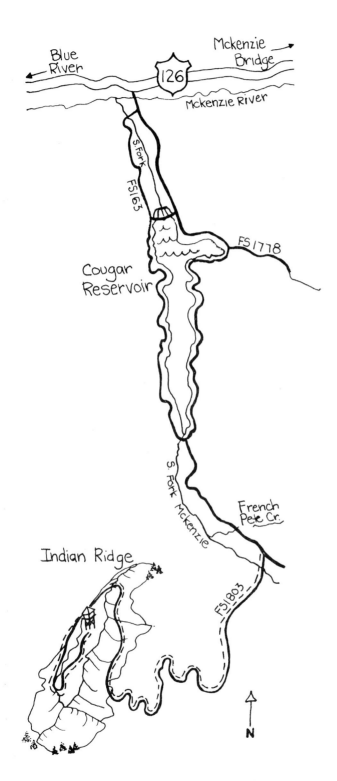

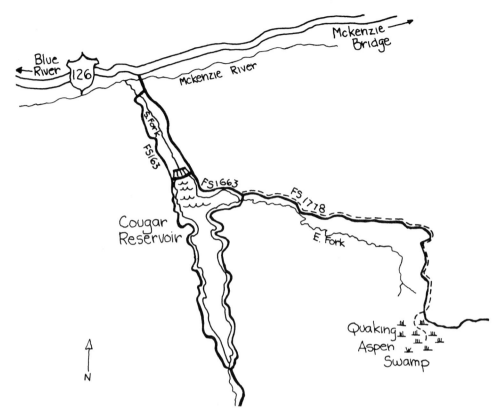

Blue River ← | 126 | McKenzie River | McKenzie Bridge →

S Fork

FS163

FS1663

FS 1718

Cougar Reservoir

E. Fork

Quaking Aspen Swamp

N

quaking aspen swamp

Road and trail tour
2-18 miles round trip
Willamette National Forest
Blue River Ranger District
Map: McKenzie Bridge Quadrangle/Blue River R.D. Fireman's Map

Quaking Aspen Swamp Botanical Area, lying east of Cougar Reservoir on the South Fork of the McKenzie River, offers a late spring tour of short duration or a mid-winter trip of overnight proportions.

The Swamp is one of the few sites where an arid-region tree, the quaking aspen, is found on the west slope of the Cascades. It is 16 miles west of the Three Sisters at the 4,400-foot level in the foothills adjacent to the French Pete Valley.

In mid-winter, tour length can be as long as 9 miles one-way. In May or June, the distance can shrink to a round-trip journey of only 2 miles — a suitable tour for a Sunday picnic or an afternoon in the sun.

To reach Quaking Aspen Swamp, drive to the community of Blue River on the McKenzie River, 38 miles east of Eugene on U.S. 126. From Blue River, proceed east on U.S. 126, and after 5 miles turn south on Forest Service Road 163, which leads to Cougar Reservoir.

Follow FS163 to the top of the dam, then turn east on FS1663, cross the dam and follow the edge of the reservoir 2 miles to the point where the East Fork of the McKenzie River enters the reservoir.

FS1778 joins FS1663 at this spot. Drive as far up FS1778 as snow conditions allow. From the reservoir, the distance to Quaking Aspen Swamp is between 9 and 10 miles. During primary winter months, a trip to the Swamp could average 14 to 18 miles round-trip, with length depending upon access.

In the spring, snow at lower elevations is usually gone by late May, with the exception of shaded sections which may persistently block traffic until well into June.

FS1778 is uphill all the way until you reach a saddle at 4,700 feet. Shortly beyond, a sign marking the trail to Quaking Aspen Swamp is visible on the south border of the roadway.

The trail, not more than one-half mile, drops some 300 feet in a series of switchbacks, and, while snow lingers long in the Swamp itself, it may often disappear from the trail sections early, in which case skis may be either cached or carried.

In addition to the aspen, other botanical attractions prosper, and can be seen turning ruffled leaves to an occasional spring sun as the snows recede from the Swamp's waterways.

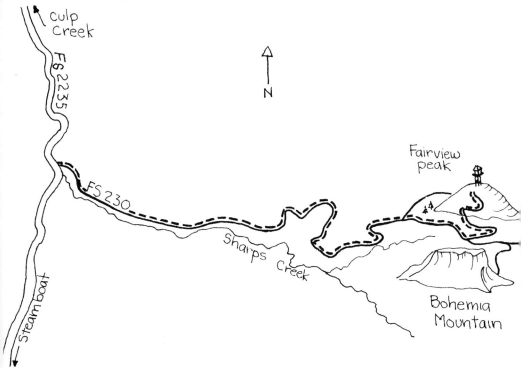

fairview peak

Road tour
10-20 miles round-trip
Umpqua National Forest
Cottage Grove Ranger District
Map: Fairview Peak Quandrangle

Fairview Peak and Bohemia Mountain offer yet another change of pace for tourers tired of the usual drive to distant mountain passes. The summit of Fairview Peak is only 31 miles east of Interstate 5.

To get there, travel east of Cottage Grove on county roads, passing Dorena Reservoir and paralleling the Row River until you reach the community of Culp Creek. Just past Culp Creek, Sharps Creek enters the Row River and the road forks. Turn south at this point, cross Row River and follow the Sharps Creek Road. The route is well-marked.

Ten miles from Culp Creek and shortly after you enter the Umpqua National Forest, the final route to the summit, a narrower track, continues up Sharps Creek as Forest Service Road 230. The high standard road continues south along Martin Creek. Drive up FS230 as far as possible.

Depending on snow level, tour distance can be anywhere from 5 to 10 miles one-way. Elevation gain is the main factor in determining difficulty. The tour route follows the canyon bottom placidly for 2 miles to Mineral Campground. It then begins climbing steeply (4,000 feet in eight switchback-ridden miles). Under powdery conditions the tour is a miraculous delight. With crust and hardpack it is a screaming horror — fit only for the foolhardy or those with metal edges.

Rich in minerals, Fairview-Bohemia contained some large veins of various metals, and mining strikes were made at the beginning of the century. Sporadic mining has progressed to the present time and over 2,000 mining claims have been staked, resulting in a hazardous maze of abandoned shafts and tunnels. Consequently, off-road skiing is not recommended. A number of open-air shafts still exist in unlikely places and such often-fun practices as cutting switchbacks on the trip down could contain unforseen hazards.

A mile before Fairview's summit, the road passes through Bohemia Saddle with Bohemia Mountain to the south. A road continues the last mile to the top of Fairview while a second road drops down in the direction of Musick Guard Station and Champion Saddle. A possible traverse down to Champion Saddle and out via the road that parallels Champion Creek would push tour length to between 15 and 20 miles and would necessitate a car shuttle.

While away from major peaks and technically a foothill, Fairview-Bohemia rises a thousand feet above its neighbors and offers an expansive view that ranges along the Cascade crest from Mt. Hood to Mt. McLoughlin and west to the Willamette Valley and Marys Peak in the coast range.

cinnamon butte

Road tour
6 miles round-trip
Umpqua National Forest
Diamond Lake Ranger District
Map: Diamond Lake Quadrangle

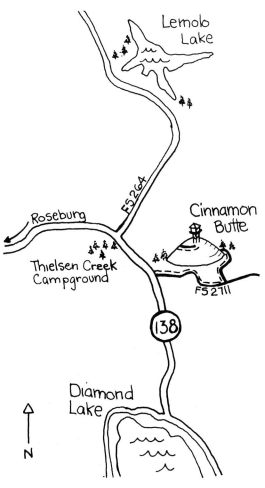

Cinnamon Butte lies north of Mt. Thielsen a few miles west of the crest of the Cascades. At an elevation of 6,417 feet it provides a stunning view of nearby Mt. Thielsen, Mt. Bailey and Diamond Lake and also rewards those individuals willing to climb to the top with an invigorating downhill run. Tour length is 3 miles one-way, with an elevation gain of 1600 feet.

To make the tour, drive east from Roseburg on Oregon 138 which follows the North Umpqua River. As soon as signs indicate you are within 10 miles of Diamond Lake, begin looking for the turn-off to Lemolo Lake and shortly beyond, Thielsen Creek Campground. The tour starts at the junction of Forest Service Road 2711 and Oregon 138. The junction is 1¾ miles beyond the Thielsen Creek Campground on the east side of the highway.

Once at the trailhead, ski up FS2711 for 2 miles, climbing moderately. Cinnamon Butte will begin to emerge on the left through the trees. A telephone line parallels the road and leads to the lookout tower on Cinnamon's summit. The final mile of road, a narrow track, veers north off FS2711 and climbs with an increased grade to the lookout.

This tour is meaningful to people who believe that the rewards for labor should equal the effort invested. The last slog up the butte, very definitely uphill, pays off with 2 long joyous miles of effortless skiing to the bottom. The road to the top, while steep in places, is open enough that a good track can be set and followed with few problems. When the snow is right, upper sections of the track offer a good ride with none of the traditional obstacles, such as tight turns or tree-wells. For tourers just becoming familiar with their skis, it is an excellent opportunity to perfect downhill touring.

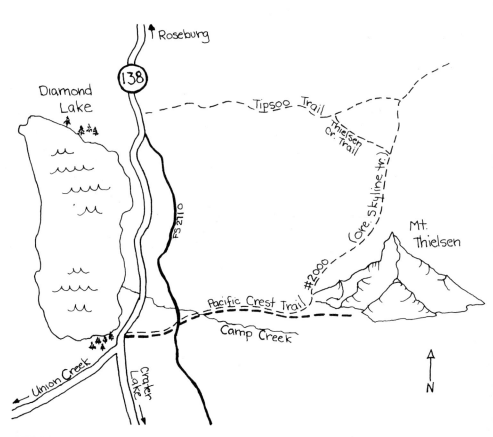

↑ Roseburg

138

Diamond Lake

Tipsoo Trail

Thielsen Cr. Trail

FS 2110

(Ore. Skyline tr.)

Mt. Thielsen

#2000

Pacific Crest Trail

Camp Creek

← Union Creek

Crater Lake →

N

mt. thielsen

Trail tour
8 miles round-trip
Umpqua National Forest
Diamond Lake Ranger District
Map: Diamond Lake Quadrangle

Mt. Thielsen is rated one of Oregon's top ten peaks in mountaineering circles. At 9,182 feet, it is a central landmark in the Diamond Lake area — an icy pinnacle scraping the sky under the harsh brightness of a winter sun.

The peak, not termed difficult for summer climbers, presents an easily accessible though more difficult target for people trying the art of winter mountaineering. Because of exposure and a characteristic build-up of ryme ice, parties attempting it should have experienced leaders.

The main appeal of Thielsen to the mountaineer and also to the tourer who wishes only to explore the lower slopes, is the relatively short approach from a plowed highway. From the starting point at the edge of Oregon 138, timberline at the 7,600-foot level is no more than 4 miles by trail.

The trail, the Pacific Crest Trail (Oregon Skyline Trail, No. 2000) begins near a trailer court at the south end of Diamond Lake and is a short distance north of South Shore Picnic Area on the east side of the highway. It is well-signed. The trail travels almost due east for one-third of a mile and crosses Forest Service Road 2710. From there the route continues east though it swings a bit north and crosses the Camp Creek drainage. The trail is moderately steep but it becomes steeper at the timberline.

From the lower slopes of Thielsen, Diamond Lake and Mt. Bailey are visible directly to the west, and if you take care good runs can be had on open slopes if conditions are favorable. As climbs go higher, conditions become icier and more windswept and less desirable for touring skis.

Once you reach timberline there are several options available. Day tourers may return on the track made coming in. Overnighters can set up snow camps with good views of the mountains and Diamond Lake. For the ambitious, a longer tour can be made by continuing on the Skyline Trail which turns north at the 7,200 foot level and skirts the mountain. Several additional trails intersect at numerous points, and different routes, depending on the inevitable variables, can be devised.

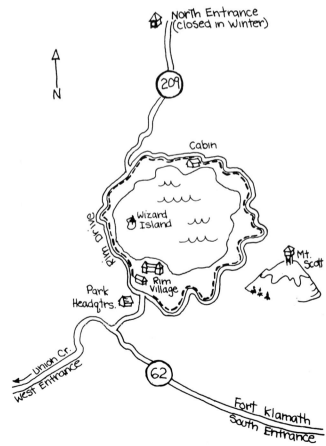

North Entrance
(Closed in Winter)

209

Cabin

N

Rim drive

Wizard
Island

Mt.
Scott

Rim
Village

Park
Headqtrs.

Union Cr.
West Entrance

62

Fort Klamath
South Entrance

crater lake national park

Road, trail and open country tours
Many tours of varying lengths
Map: Crater Lake National Park

Ski touring at Crater Lake is a unique experience. It can offer both tours of a few hours or longer trips of several days duration. One primary feature of touring in the park is non-fluctuating however; tell the rangers where you are going.

Touring in the Crater Lake area has a number of dangers, but the most feared by Park Service personnel is the continual danger of individuals walking, skiing, snowshoeing, etc., over cornices and into the lake. It is a very real danger and they will emphasize it when talking to you.

Once you have demonstrated awareness of this and other problems, the Park Service personnel are most helpful. While day tours emanate in a number of directions from the Crater Lake Lodge on the southwest side of the lake, longer trips, including the much publicized tour around the lake's rim (34 miles), can also be made.

The rim tour, usually done in two or more days, is perhaps best attempted during spring months when weather is consistently good for long periods. During late spring, however, a problem with blowing volcanic grit can slow down touring speed noticeably and gives snow in exposed places a consistency somewhat akin to sandpaper.

A nice feature of the rim tour is the availability of a cabin located approximately half way around at the 16 mile point. The cabin, in the past generally available to groups, has an enclosed, chimney-like entrance-way which is reachable even after deep snows. Arrangements can be made for the cabin's use by contacting the Park Service

prior to your arrival at the park on the scheduled day of the tour.

You can pick up the key at Park headquarters. Information regarding up-to-date weather conditions is available.

By beginning on the west side of the lake near Crater Lake Lodge and skiing west, you will find the first half of the trip around the rim fairly straightforward, though road-cuts in the vicinity of the Watchman Lookout could pose problems. On the second half of the tour you may encounter some severe problems with snowed-over road-cuts. Park Service advice as to the best routes to negotiate these obstacles would be well taken.

Whatever the tour at Crater Lake, the elevation — consistently above 6,000 feet — makes for excellent snow conditions much of the winter. The lake, an often photographed spectacle in its winter finery, is a sight of beauty not easily forgotten.

steens mountain

Open country touring
18 miles average (25 miles longest)
Bureau of Land Management
Maps: Available from BLM, Burns,
Oregon

Steens Mountain, located south of Burns in the high desert country of southeastern Oregon, offers some of the finest spring skiing available in the state. This is a land of wide open spaces. Glorious long ridges, their sagebrush and juniper covered by 10 feet of snow, sparkle in the radiance of fresh April mornings.

Ski touring in the Steens is *not* for everyone. To begin with, access is a problem. To get there, drive to Burns, then south 60 miles to the town of Frenchglen, a noteworthy attraction on its own merits. Frenchglen is the end of the line: a store, gas station, school, hotel and road maintenance station. The hotel, incidentally, is a famed attraction in the area and people planning on staying there should call ahead for reservations. Trips to the Malheur Wildlife Refuge located outside of town along the Donner and Blitzen River bring many visitors to the area, and space is not always available.

Ski touring in the vicinity exists about 10 to 18 miles east of town, depending on the time of the year and the snow level. A road, primarily on Bureau of Land Management land, travels east 18 miles to Fish Lake (7,000 feet elevation). From Frenchglen drive east toward Fish Lake as far as possible. The route is well-signed. You will eventually be stopped by either snow, mud or incredible ruts. The road is not maintained in winter and travellers venture forth at their own risk. Sudden storms are always possible in the area, and a blizzard can lay down a large amount of snow in a short time. Consequently, the potential for getting a vehicle stuck in the area does exist and should be considered.

You must also consider the skill levels of the party involved. This is not a day tour. It is also not a tour for those who are inexperienced in winter camping or in winter travel in general. While the road to Fish Lake is often discernible, it is easy to lose and, in whiteout conditions, every rolling ridge looks like another. You should definitely carry map and compass, and should know how to use them.

From the vehicles, wherever parked, the route progresses gently upward and often the climbing is barely noticeable. As you near Fish Lake, ridges become steeper and more pronounced, and the lake itself actually lies in a pocket amongst several gently sloping backbones — a noticeable flat spot which can't be missed. In summer, the area is a much-used summer recreation site and a number of outhouses dot the shoreline.

There are also several cabins in the area, one belonging to BLM and the others to the Oregon State Game Commission. These are not open to the public. Water is available near the Game Commission structure, a green A-frame, via a pipe from a year-round spring about 20 feet from the building. The A-frame is about one-half mile northwest of Fish Lake.

Accommodations in the area are entirely up to the individual. Because of good snow conditions and the severity of wind in the area, a large snow cave is often the best solution. Mountain tents are also appropriate but are not as much protection in driving snow.

To conclude, this is a country for the experienced cross-country skier and winter outdoorsman. Long, rolling ridges abound and may be followed eastward. Steens Mountain summit, at 9,670 feet offering a panoramic view of the surrounding country, drops off to the Alvord Desert far below on the east side. You are completely on your own. Once you establish a base camp, the only limit on tours is personal stamina and imagination.

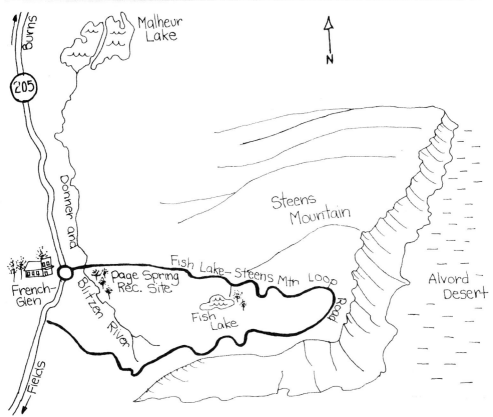

glossary

This is a list of terms used by Oregon ski tourers. Some may seem similar to downhill skiers' terms, but it is the downhill skier who acquired them from the ski tourer years ago.

Birdback — A Forest service wooden mounting bracket for Smokey Bear posters usually found at all trailheads.

To break trail — To lead off on a touring trip.

Clearcut — A logged-over section of forest where all the trees were cut in a given patch, block or unit. May be called a clearcut unit or harvest area.

Crust — Hard snow surface.

Easy-chair sportsman — Individual who runs a snowmobile.

Fireman's Map — Forest Service road maps.

Freeski — A catchphrase having the connotation of independence, no organizational restrictions, no restricted areas.

Oregon snow — Poor quality snow usually wet and requiring a sticky sort of wax. "Idaho green" means good powdery snow. It gets the name from the use of green wax which is the hardest wax there is.

Pitchwood — Generally describes wood full of pitch but applied to anything used as fire-starter.

Poling — Keeping skis together on a slight slope and shoving with poles.

Snow bridge — An arch of snow crossing a stream, not necessarily safe.

Step turn — Picking up one ski while going downhill, stepping in a slightly different direction and shifting weight to bring other ski in line.

Sink — Pot-hole, rock or log hidden just below surface.

Trailhead — Beginning point of trip.

Traverse — Method of going downhill or uphill by slow switchbacks.

Undercut — Where water has left a snowbridge across a creek that looks incapable of supporting the weight of the unwary.

Uphill glider, easy slider — Ski tourer or cross-country skier.

Virgin snow — Any undisturbed snow area.

Wands — Bamboo or metal sticks with plastic tape flags used to mark a course or trail not well-defined.

Whiteout — Light condition caused by a blending of snow and clouds that eliminates shadows and makes it almost impossible to see.

157

index

Photography: Douglas Newman with Oscar Palmquist assisting in technical production

Cinnamon Butte photo: Mike Hughes
Quaking Aspen Swamp: Leslie Childress

Maps: Susan Scovell
Book Design: Sally Sharrard